"*Unknown Rider* is the best book I've ever read...and I'm not kidding."

—*Shaun Germain, Aviation Enthusiast, Age 14*

"This book is important for the young—to follow their dreams, and for us older people—to show us that the horizon is still unlimited. As a person who has flown in the F-16, I wish I had read this book first. God bless all the air defenders who protect our country today!"

—*Elizabeth Strohfus, Women's Air Force Service Pilot—WWII, Age 76*

"I've never read a book that captured a pilot's life so well. It brings back so many great memories, it makes me want to go back through training my-self."

—*Lieutenant Colonel Jim Ed Green, Commander, 159th Fighter Group*
and former F-16 Instructor, USAF Fighter Weapons School

"*[Unknown Rider]* is really a must-read book for any young person inter-ested in aviation."

—*Ed Lachendro, Executive Director, EAA Young Eagles Program*

To DAD
From SUSIE,
JOHN, KIDS

Unknown RIDER

by Scott Anderson

with illustrations by Andrea Dwyer

DENNOCH PRESS

Duluth, Minnesota

Dennoch Press
808 Martha Street
Duluth, Minnesota 55805
218-728-0505 / 800-336-6624

Unknown Rider

© 1995 by Scott D. Anderson. All rights reserved. Except for short excerpts for review purposes, no part of this book may be reproduced or transmitted in any form by any means electronic or mechanical without permission in writing from the publisher.

This novel is a work of fiction. Names, characters, places, and incidents are either the product of the author's imagination or are used fictitiously. Any resemblance to actual events, locales, organizations or persons, living or dead, is entirely coincidental and beyond the intent of either the author or the publisher.

Excerpts taken from: "Why Do We Fly" from *West with the Night* by Beryl Markham. Copyright 1942, 1983 by Beryl Markham. Reprinted by permission of North Point Press, a division of Farrar, Straus & Giroux, Inc. *Rabble in Arms* by Kenneth Roberts. Copyright 1933, 1947 by Kenneth Roberts. Used by permission of Doubleday, a division of Bantam Doubleday Dell Publishing Group, Inc. *More Poems* by A.E. Housman. Copyright 1936 by Barclays Bank, Ltd. Copyright 1964 by Robert E. Symons. Reprinted by permission of Henry Holt and Co., Inc.

Printed in the United States of America by Bang Printing.
10 9 8 7 6 5 4 3 2 1

Cover by Jeff Brownell
Illustrations by Andrea Dwyer
Layout by Tony Dierckins

ISBN 0-9644521-0-3

To the Guard Bums and the Gas Stooges,
and to Matt, who made me into both.

Contents

Acknowledgments

WHEN I WAS TRAINING TO FLY the F-16 at Kingsley Field in Oregon, each evening, after a day of flying fighters, I sat down and typed a little bit of this book. I probably should have spent more time studying and less time at the keyboard. But I couldn't keep from writing. The elements of a story were all around me: mountains, farms, cropdusters, old guys with rundown hangars, grass strips, concrete runways, beat-up old taildraggers and, of course, supersonic fighters. It couldn't have been any easier. All I had to do was invent a few characters, put them in an airplane, and make them the heroes of the stories that filled the air.

More difficult was making the stories into a book. For this I am indebted to a great many people. Among them are Larry Fortner, Dick Fish, Steven Schwarze, Betty Courier, Diana Johnson, Kirk Madson, and Terry Schroth. The value of their contributions cannot be exaggerated.

I am equally grateful to Andrea Dwyer. Her illustrations and ideas changed the face of this book. Someday I'm going to learn how to draw. Until then, I plan on keeping her phone number handy.

And then there are the pilots—John Fulton, Pat Macatee, Monte Preston, Dan Lewis, and Dave Marconi. If it hadn't been for them, I believe I would have lived a normal, decent life. But I never would have flown a Champ. I never would have been a fighter pilot. If it hadn't been for them, I never would have known the stories that make up this book.

A pilot's life is a wonderful life. I hope I've done it justice.

Scott Anderson
Duluth, Minnesota

Prologue

THERE EXISTS WITHIN THIS COUNTRY a little-known and largely misunderstood group of people who spend their lives just a few yards from armed fighter jets, ready to take to the sky in defense of America.

At the height of the Cold War, 2,000 aircraft and 100 fighter squadrons were assigned the mission of Air Defense. Today, just ten squadrons perform this role. Each squadron supports an Air Defense Alert site on the perimeter of the United States. At each site two fighters maintain Alert status 24 hours a day, 365 days a year.

Two pilots wait at each site, ready to fly at any time, in any weather. They are the best-trained, best-equipped, best-supported air defenders in the world. Their mission? To intercept, identify and, if necessary, engage and destroy airborne intruders that pose a threat to national security.

They are America's first and last line of defense. They are all that stand between you and the rest of the world.

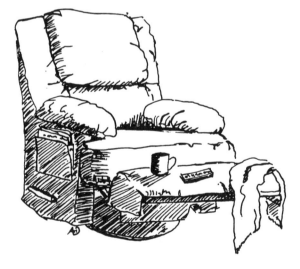

CHAPTER I

The Klaxon

So, he scolded, now it has come to this. To walk is not enough.
To ride a horse is not enough. Now people must ride
from place to place through the air like a dika toorin.
Nothing but trouble will come of it.

— Beryl Markam, *West with the Night*

Uₙₖₙₒwₙ Rᵢₑₙ, Uₙₖₙₒwₙ Rᵢₑₙ."

The young man jumped from his plush blue recliner and stared wide-eyed at the small speaker perched atop the room's big-screen television.

Again the command to the unidentified aircraft that had entered American airspace: "Unknown Rider, Unknown Rider, one hundred ten miles south of Cigar tracking three-six-zero, two hundred knots, this is Oakgrove on Guard; recycle all transponder modes and contact Oakgrove on two three five decimal one."

The procedure for this situation was clear-cut. Oakgrove, the Southeast Air Defense Sector radar control team, had two minutes to identify the aircraft. If it could not, the sector commander would scramble the F-16s on Alert at Florida's Tyndall Air Force Base to intercept it.

For most people sleeping peacefully under the umbrella of the Southeast Air Defense Sector, the next two minutes would pass uneventfully. But not for Lieutenant Rick Wedan. He was the young man who had been sitting peacefully in the recliner. He was one of the Air Defense pilots, sitting Alert for the first time in his life. And all he had on was his underwear.

To make matters worse, Rick's flight lead—Captain Dave Allen—was in the shower.

Powered by the adrenaline surging through his veins, Rick dashed to the bathroom and pounded on its half-open door. "Second Unknown Rider!" he shouted, his voice rising half an octave with each word.

The senior pilot, his head full of shampoo, leaned out of the shower and wiped the suds from his eyes. "What?"

"Second Unknown Rider!"

In an instant Dave was a blur of shower-pink skin, tracking soap, shampoo, and water across the bathroom, down the short hallway, and into the adjacent bedroom.

Rick was right behind, racing to get dressed before the horn went off for the scramble. If, in fact, they were going to scramble.

He ran to where he had placed his flying gear. There, neatly laid out on the floor as if by his mother for his first day of school, were his socks, his parachute harness complete with inflatable life preserver, his chap-like g-suit pants, his Nomex flightsuit, and his black leather flying boots.

Dave had told him that the secret to going fast was to go slow. A pilot in a panic, he had warned, puts his boots on before his flightsuit. Rick could see how that could cause a problem. So he intended to stay calm. And he did. Right up until the air exploded around his head.

"ERRRRRRRRRRRR!" The Klaxon scramble horn.

* * *

A modern Klaxon can have quite an effect on a person trying to go slow to go fast while at the same time trying very hard not to panic. Unlike its World War II predecessors, cranked by hand from the tops of wooden towers, the modern thousand-megawatt turboelectric Klaxon doesn't wail—it blares. It blares so loudly, so urgently, and so horribly that if one were accidentally turned on at something even as peaceful as a softball game, the stands would empty within seconds as players and fans alike scrambled for their imaginary jets.

The antithesis of wake-to-music and the snooze button, the modern Klaxon was developed through years of research by sleep scientists, psychologists, dentists, and tax collectors. The sound is the piercing cry of a baby, the spinal chill of fingernails down a blackboard, and the awful pain of a root canal all wrapped into one. Its purpose is to get a dozing pilot out of bed, dressed, and into a cockpit ready to fly—all within the allotted five minutes. And it does just that—often long before the pilot is actually awake.

If the Klaxon can do this to a person sleeping soundly, imagine what it can do to a person already wide awake. Before Rick knew it, he had his flightsuit on, his boots laced, and his g-suit snapped around his waist. He had just closed the g-suit zipper on one leg when he saw Dave streak past the door, wearing all his equipment and just a little white foam behind his right ear.

The sight inspired Rick. To heck with going slow. He yanked down the zipper on his other leg, grabbed his parachute harness, and bolted for the door.

* * *

Parked just outside the living quarters were the Alert bicycles. Antique products of a different age, these single-speed machines reduced the travel time from the recliners to the jets. After years of duty, the bicycles had been bent and twisted so badly by pilots slamming them into the wall at the end of the fifty-yard race to the jets that driving them in a straight line was next to impossible. This, coupled with the fact that they were geared low enough to tow semi-trailers, left riding the bikes one of the most dangerous phases of the scramble. Most of the pilots were at least mildly afraid of the contraptions, particularly at night and especially in the rain.

Rick had yet to learn this fear. Without hesitation he grabbed his mount from the rack and pedaled away, into the rain, into the night. He headed for his F-16, tail number 787. It lay in the nearer of the two floodlit Alert hangars waiting for him to bring it life.

Pedaling madly, Rick coaxed every ounce of hurry he could from his aged bike. Like a retriever so intent on catching a stick that it disregards the backyard fence it is about to hit, Rick didn't think to slow before reaching the hangar. Instead, he waited until the last second and then hit the brakes as hard as he could.

That was when he realized why nobody liked riding the bikes in the rain. The brakes stopped the tire, but the tire didn't stop the bike. Luckily, the distance to the wall was equal to the length of wet pavement required to skid the bike to a speed at which it could be safely jettisoned. Which is exactly what Rick did, jumping off his unstable mount just before it struck the hangar wall. The bike lay there, its front tire bent but still spinning, as Rick sprinted for his jet.

Rick's crew chief, Sergeant Ray Felix, was already standing by the aircraft as Rick raced up the ladder and jumped in the cockpit. As soon as Rick was in, Sergeant Felix pulled the ladder from the jet and shouted, "Clear!" Rick reached down with his left hand, moved the main power switch to "on" and flipped the toggle switch marked "JFS" to the "Start 1" position. Hydraulic fluid under 3,000 pounds of pressure poured into the JFS (Jet Fuel Starter).

While the JFS was spooling up, Rick pulled on his gloves, turned to his right, and lifted his helmet off the canopy rail. He put it on and snapped the chin strap in place. Now he could communicate with Sergeant Felix, whose headset was plugged into a jack on the side of the jet.

Rick flipped the canopy switch. By the time the glass bubble closed over his head, the JFS had spooled the engine to the required 20 percent rpm. Rick put his hand on the throttle and lifted it over the "off" detent into "idle."

In the few seconds before the engine lit and the main generator kicked on line, Rick began strapping himself in. First the shoulder harnesses leading to the parachute inside the ejection seat, then the lap belt, then the seat kit straps connecting him to the survival kit on which he was sitting.

Finally, Rick reached up and connected the oxygen mask hanging off the right side of his helmet. As soon as it was over his mouth, the mask imploded. He couldn't breathe!

For an instant Rick thought he must have forgotten to hook up his oxygen hose when he brought his helmet out to the jet earlier that day. Then he realized the real problem. It wasn't his mask; it was his breathing. He was inhaling so hard that the air supply valve simply couldn't keep up. With great effort, Rick forced himself to relax.

"Looks like a good light," Sergeant Felix called over the intercom. Rick focused on the instruments. Everything looked normal. Forty-five percent—main generator coming on line. Fifty percent—JFS off. Fifty-five percent—engine warning light off.

Rick initiated the jet's flight control computer self-test. The flaperons, stabilators, and rudder began rocking away.

Just as Rick finished connecting his g-suit's air supply line, Dave checked him in on the VHF radio reserved for interflight communication. "Tundra check Victor," came Dave's voice.

Rick keyed his three-position radio switch and tried to speak clearly and calmly into the microphone within his oxygen mask. "Two."

Dave's voice came again, this time checking in with the Tyndall command post on the UHF radio. "Raymond Ten, Tundra Zero-One. Confirm status."

"Tundra Zero-One, this is Raymond Ten. Status is Active Air Scramble. Repeat: Active Air Scramble."

"Copy scramble," replied Dave.

"Tundra push two." Dave was directing Rick to switch the UHF radio to the preset frequency of Tyndall tower. Rick turned the radio's rotary dial until the counter read "2."

"Tundra check."

Rick moved the transmit switch aft. "Two."

"Tower, Tundra scramble two vipers."

"Tundra, you're cleared for takeoff," the tower replied. "Turn left heading one-six-zero. Climb and maintain flight level three-five-zero."

"Tundra's rolling," replied Dave as he taxied out of the hangar next to Rick.

This was it. Rick looked down to see that the flight control panel was clear; the computers had passed the test. The Inertial Navigation System was blinking; its one-and-a-half minute alignment was complete. Rick twisted the Inertial Navigation Function switch to the NAV position, confirmed proper emergency power unit operation, and gave Sergeant Felix a thumbs up. The crew chief pulled the chocks, returned the thumbs up, and saluted smartly. Rick saluted back, released his feet from the brakes, and pulled the jet out of the hangar and into the rain.

* * *

By the time Rick was out of the Alert hangar, Dave was on the runway ready for takeoff. To keep up, Rick raced down the short Alert taxiway, barely keeping all three wheels on the ground as he made the dogleg turn onto the runway. Dave's afterburner lit as Rick was arming his ejection seat. Even from within his cockpit, he could feel the power of Dave's turbofan jet engine.

Rick hacked the clock next to his right knee.

Five seconds.

Rick pushed the throttle up to 80 percent, holding the brakes while he checked the engine instruments.

Ten seconds.

Rick checked again to see that he was strapped in.

Fifteen seconds.

Rick looked up to see the twenty-foot orange flame from Dave's afterburner disappear into the black clouds.

Twenty seconds.

Rick released his brakes and shoved the throttle all the way forward to military power. The jet began to roll. Rick glanced at the engine instruments. The oil pressure looked good. The exhaust temperature looked good. The nozzle was properly closed. Satisfied, he lifted the throttle over the military power detent and pushed it up to full afterburner. The engine roared. The fighter surged ahead. As each of the five afterburner segments lit, Rick felt the acceleration build. The first fifty knots took almost five seconds—the second fifty just a couple.

At 100 knots Rick disengaged the nosewheel steering, controlling the jet now with only the airflow over the rudder. At 140 knots he eased back on the stick. At 155 knots the nosewheel lifted off the ground, and Lieutenant Richard W. Wedan entered the sky to meet the Unknown Rider.

CHAPTER II

The Champ

A man without a purpose is lost in chaos. He does not know how to judge. He cannot tell what is or is not important to him, and, therefore, he drifts helplessly at the mercy of any chance stimulus or any whim of the moment. He spends his life searching for some value which he cannot find.

—Ayn Rand

LIKE MOST RED-BLOODED AMERICAN YOUTHS weaned on World War II movies and comic books, Rick Wedan had wanted to be a fighter pilot for as long as he could remember. In fact, within the strange reality of childhood, Rick actually *had* been a fighter pilot for as long as he could remember.

Early on, along with the rest of his friends, Rick had also been a firefighter and police officer. Later, under pressure from his family and the influence of mass media, Rick became a professional football star. Eventually, his athletic career opened doors for him into the fast-paced worlds of corporate finance and espionage. To many eight-year-olds these would have been impossible occupations. To a world-renowned concert pianist and arctic explorer like Rick, however, they were just jobs.

Inevitably, the course of time removed Rick's many responsibilities one by one. In tenth grade, with the encouragement of his music teacher, Rick ended his career as a pianist. In eleventh grade, Rick turned in his secret agent credentials and closed his successful law and medical practices. By the end of high school, while those around him were reveling in the possibilities of going off and actually becoming something, Rick was facing the realization that there were many things he would never become. Yet, through it all, one shingle remained hanging over the dimly lit sidewalk of his childhood dreams. It read *Rick Wedan, Fighter Pilot.*

* * *

Though by the time he entered college Rick already considered himself an accomplished and heroic pilot, his aviation development to that point had been somewhat stymied by the fact that he had never actually flown an airplane.

Enter Matthew J. Schuster.

If Rick's background was a model of the norm, Matt's was a model of the aberrant, at least according to Matt. "My father," Matt once wrote as a child, "was a fighter pilot. He crash-landed his P-51 on the same day he shot down five Germans. He never would have crashed except he was trying to save his best friend. My mother was a stripper in the USO before becoming a spy. She used her training to get behind enemy lines and steal secret plans for German jet fighters. She got captured while trying to escape in her motorcar across the mountains."

The fantasy wasn't entirely without basis. Matt's father *had* participated in the Second World War. He had been an engineer with the Seabees. Matt's mother *had* for a time worked as a stripper—at an Oakland dry dock, removing paint from battleships. Later she joined the Women's Air Force at Avenger Field in Houston as a B-25 ferry pilot. She met Matt's father at a USO dance in California near the end of the war. The two were married three months later at Alameda Naval Air Station. Eventually they left California and moved to upstate New York where Matt's father started what would become a prosperous construction business. The Schusters had two children, Mark in 1955 and Matt in 1964.

In 1968, Matt's father was killed in a plane crash on the way back to New York from San Francisco. Eight years later, Matt's mother died in an automobile accident in New Hampshire's White Mountains.

After his mother's death, twelve-year-old Matt was sent to the small town of Post Mills, Vermont, where his brother Mark resided when not away on business. Matt's mother had often taken him to Post Mills to visit Mark. Much of their time on these visits had been spent watching the airplanes take off and land on the town's grass strip. Sometimes, when the air was particularly clear or the colors of the leaves especially brilliant, his mother had made arrangements to rent one of the airport's little yellow J-3 Cubs and take Matt flying.

Matt stayed in Post Mills for six years—splitting his time evenly between hanging around the airport, getting his high school diploma, and generally rejecting the lessons of reality that life was teaching those around him.

The year he turned eighteen, with the blessing of his brother and in accordance with the terms of his parents' estate, Matt left Post Mills and made his way to Palo Alto, California—to college and into Rick's life—as that most influential of people, a freshman roommate.

* * *

Rick's first day with Matt was a harbinger of things to come. While their new classmates were unpacking their student be-longings, Matt and Rick were driving to the local airport—at Matt's suggestion but in Rick's car—just to check things out.

The ramp of fancy late-model airplanes they found inter-ested Matt not at all. What did catch his eye was a small, rag-gedy, cloth-covered, single-engine relic standing all by itself.

A young man clad in dirty blue jeans, tennis shoes, and a red-and-black flannel lumberjack shirt was standing at the front of the plane. Shocks of jet-black hair hung from under his red baseball cap.

As Matt and Rick watched, the man grasped the propeller, braced his feet on the tarmac, and tensed his body. Summoning all his strength, he gave the blade a fierce pull. The propeller rotated, coughed through one revolution, then jerked to a stop.

Rick parked the car. Matt got out and started toward the ramp. His eyes were fixed on the airplane. His mind was traveling to another scene.

"Try it again!" his mother yelled out the open door. Matt reached up once more and grabbed the propeller. It was the middle of September, and though the sun was bright in the Vermont sky, the autumn chill was setting in, and the long, thin steel blade was cold against his unprotected fingers.

He threw the full weight of his twelve-year-old body into it this time, pulling the aged engine through its cycle while his mother moved the throttle back and forth, trying to find the one special position that would bring the engine life.

The engine coughed, then caught. Matt instinctively backed away from the whirling propeller. Then, like a cat, he ran to the airplane's door and jumped into the seat in front of his mother. "Keep the stick back in your lap," she called over the engine, which was now humming away in a low, solid rhythm. "Keep the tailwheel down so you can steer..."

Matt ran toward the airplane. As he got close, the engine caught and the plane's one-man ground and flight crew jumped into its cockpit just as it began to roll away. Soon it was down the runway and airborne.

Even from a distance it was clear that something was not quite right with the airplane. With Rick in tow, Matt jogged the few yards to the airport office to find out what it was.

"Oh, that's the Champ," the man behind the counter answered. "It's a little odd, all right. Belongs to John Macatee. John does some instructing here, but he keeps the Champ tied up over at Skysailing."

"Skysailing?" asked Matt.

"It's kind of an airport over in Fremont. It's really just the remnant of a horse racing track waiting for the right developer to scoop it up. But they do some soaring out of it. John likes keeping the Champ there. Something about no control tower or inspectors being around. It's not far. He's probably heading over there now."

At Matt's insistence, the man scribbled some directions on the back of an airport brochure.

* * *

At Skysailing, which sounded much better than it looked, Matt and Rick found several airplanes tied down next to a dilapidated stable with a *For Sale* sign in the window. The Champ, however, was nowhere to be seen. Neither was the runway. All they could make out was an old horsetrack, a couple small fields of weeds, and the long, straight pothole-riddled road on which they were driving.

The sight of the airborne Champ coming straight at them and the realization of the truth occurred almost simultaneously. The long gravel strip they were on wasn't a road—it was a runway. And they were about to get hit!

In a panic, Rick veered the car off the gravel and onto the grass. Once safely clear, the two new roommates looked back at the odd little Champ, which, in eerie silence, was gliding in for a landing. After a perfect touchdown, the airplane rolled a few hundred feet over the grass and gravel, then came to a stop next to their car. Out jumped John Macatee, the young man they had seen at Palo Alto.

John gave Matt and Rick a grin and waved. "Boy," he said, "I'm glad you got out of the way. The engine quit a couple miles out and I only had one shot at the landing."

"Sorry," returned Matt, "we didn't know it was a runway."

"No problem," said John, "I'm just glad I didn't have to land on the car."

Matt stepped forward to help push the airplane clear of the runway. Rick followed. As they got closer, Rick found himself squinting at the aircraft with one eye open and the other half closed, trying vainly to get the proper perspective on it. At first Rick thought his inability to get a clear take on the craft stemmed from its many colors. But now he could see that it wasn't the colors that distorted the picture. It was the shape.

"Your plane seen a little damage?" Rick asked.

The flier shook his head. "No," he answered, "never been damaged."

Matt eyed the plane, then the pilot.

"Okay," he admitted, "never damaged beyond repair."

All three laughed.

* * *

After introductions, John explained that he didn't own the Champ. It belonged to a guy named Ace Bigby. John had flown fire patrol for Ace that summer up in Oregon. John had loved flying the Champ around the fire base so much that though Ace couldn't bring himself to sell the craft—due more to legal than sentimental reasons—he had let John borrow it indefinitely as part of his pay.

"A few years ago," said John as he opened up the cowling and started tugging at the bird's nest of wires inside, "Ace messed up one of the wings a little bit on his way to some crazy airstrip in a river canyon. Rather than rebuild it, he decided to just replace it with a Super Cub wing he had from another wreck. The gear needed a little work, too, so he modified a set from an old Stinson—at least the left gear. The right one is original. Other than that, and I guess the new bigger engine and gas tanks, everything is pretty standard. Except the seats. I think he got them out of some tractors after the incident in the lake. It flies great, though. Once you get the hang of it."

By this time John had finished messing with the engine wires and had snapped the cowling closed. "That should do it," he said with a grin. "Say, you guys want to go get some gas so we can take 'er up for a spin?"

* * *

Their response to that question marked the beginning of Rick's and Matt's lives as gas stooges—a name John applied loosely to anyone who put a couple bucks worth of gas in the Champ's tank in exchange for flying privileges. As gas stooges, Matt and Rick were entitled to half the flying time during a trip. More importantly, they were entitled to free instruction in such necessary Champ skills as Duct Tape Fabric Repair and Solo By-Hand Engine Starting. John also taught them how to appear properly forlorn by the side of the road when trying to hitchhike from an airport to a gas station to fill the jerry cans with relatively inexpensive car gas.

Actually, John hated carrying the dented old cans in the Champ. The rusting containers leaked, and the gas that seeped through invisible cracks filled the small cockpit with nauseating fumes. In addition, carrying the cans eliminated the need for John's favorite Champ challenge—finding gas stations on old gravel roads, landing the airplane next to them, and filling up right there. Inasmuch as there were certain obvious logistical problems with this kind of refueling, however, the cans usually went in back, along with tools, hats, gloves, jackets, and sleeping bags for the inevitable nights spent in the Champ, under its wing, or on a hangar floor.

* * *

The most extended Champ trip of all came three years after Rick and Matt met John. The summer after their junior year, while their more prudent friends were laboring away at career-building internships, Matt and Rick joined John on what their instructor called the "Cross Country"—a journey that had been taking shape in his somewhat twisted mind for quite some time.

For John, the Cross Country was more than simply a way to justify a few weeks of unemployment. It was a graphic representation of his personal plan for addressing what he considered the greatest injustice in the nation—the admissions policy for Air Force Pilot Training.

John's feelings on the subject ran deep. His outstanding college Reserve Officer Training Corps performance and thousands of hours of flying time notwithstanding, John had been unable to qualify for a pilot slot in the Air Force due to a minor anomaly in his left eye. On various occasions over three years he had taken the Air Force physical, trying everything from exercising his eyes for hours every day to memorizing hundreds of Air Force eye charts in futile efforts to pass the test. In the end, he had resorted to changing the test results on his examination papers when the ophthalmologist left the room. He had been caught, and those in charge had not looked kindly upon his resourcefulness. As a result, he had been rejected as an Air Force pilot candidate. For the wrong reason, John insisted.

"The Air Force spends way too much time and money worrying about a pilot's physical qualifications," John often lamented. "What they ought to worry about are his flying qualifications. It would be a lot better if, instead of all the stupid tests and physicals and stuff, they just brought all pilot applicants to Skysailing, equipped each of them with a Champ, fifty dollars cash, an atlas, and a Vise Grip and let them go. Whoever showed up in Lubec within a month would be in."

John had never been to Lubec. But in the atlas, Lubec, Maine, looked like the farthest point from Skysailing that a person could fly and still remain in the continental United States.

It was John's determination to put his own skills to this test that prompted the Cross Country. Matt and Rick were to go along as proctors. In exchange for a month of uninterrupted instruction, all they had to do was verify to the world that the trip had been completed. That, and supply the fifty dollars, the Vise Grip, and the atlas.

The plan didn't sound especially safe, but it did sound extremely exciting. So, one fine spring day when their classes were finally out, Matt and Rick traded their books and calculators for lumberjack shirts, jeans, and baseball caps, helped John strain two cans of auto gas into the Champ through an old felt hat, and headed east.

CHAPTER III

Wawa

It made me somehow feel that
I had missed the chance to do great things.

— Kenneth Roberts, *Rabble in Arms*

IN ADDITION TO DEMONSTRATING the value of John's plan for screening Air Force pilot candidates, the Cross Country was notable for three reasons. First, the flight included three people in a two-person airplane. Second, it was made without benefit of licenses on the part of Rick and Matt or insurance on the part of John—two formalities held to be essential in today's flying world. Third, and most important, it was on the Cross Country that Rick met Dangerous Dave Allen. And after that, nothing was ever really the same.

They were two weeks and nearly two thousand miles into the trip when they met up with Dave. They had crossed the Sierras. They had crossed the Rockies. They had flown five feet above the Montana plains and scouted coyotes. On through South Dakota they had traveled, flying as long as the light held out, stopping only if the headwind exceeded their airspeed. They were traveling east, with the prevailing winds, so that happened only rarely.

They had touched down once in Minnesota, just long enough to fill up on gas at the farm town of Brownton sixty miles west of Minneapolis. Then they had pressed on, passing just fifty or

so miles south of Rick's hometown of Duluth on their way to
Michigan's Upper Peninsula. Rick had lobbied hard to stop in
Duluth to partake in all the comforts that home might afford,
but his plea had been ignored by John. There were rules to be
followed, John explained. Without rules, the trip would be
meaningless.

So, instead of spending the night in soft beds in Duluth,
Rick, Matt, and John spent it on the hard floor of an abandoned
house trailer parked next to the unmowed grass field on which
they had landed.

* * *

The next morning Rick pushed open the trailer's ill-fitting door
to view a thick sky. The ceiling was low and rain hung in the
air. It looked like a day they'd be spending in the trailer. Rick
called his observation in to John. A few minutes later, John's
head popped out of the doorway. He rubbed his eyes and looked
at the sky. "I thought you said we couldn't fly," he said. "Heck,
I can see the Champ from here."

The previous day, John had been relegated to squeezing
into the back tractor seat with Matt while Rick got some stick
time in the front. This day it was John's turn to take the front
seat and the primary controls.

Lumbering down the runway, the Champ spun a long
rooster-tail of water behind it off the rain-soaked grass. As the
plane accelerated, its tail became airborne at the command of
the stick John was holding in the full-forward position. Five seconds later, John eased back on the stick, and the Champ came
alive, freeing them once again from the earth and all its unnatu-
ral restraints to movement.

The instant the wheels broke ground, the three pilots became lords over the planet beneath them. If, on the ground,
they had seen a beautiful estate on rolling green acres, they
would have been able only to walk to its fence and poke their

noses through in admiration. From the air, it was *their* mansion. They could fly above it. They could fly to one side. They could do barrel rolls for its entire length and then, without reason or circumstance, they could fly away. They didn't have to pay taxes or care for maintenance. It was ownership of a higher sort—without deeds or titles.

This ownership didn't apply only to mansions, or towns, or cities. It applied to the earth—to fields and forests and mountains. It applied to islands and rivers. It applied to lakes.

That morning it was to a lake that they flew. Lake Superior. The world's greatest lake. Full of cold, clear water and ringed by shoreline more rugged and beautiful than any on earth.

But the Champ team headed to the lake that day for practical, not aesthetic reasons. With the thick clouds only a few hundred feet above the ground, they would have to do some low flying—some *scud-running*. Over land this would mean keeping a vigilant lookout for radio towers and powerlines. Over the water, following the shoreline, they would encounter no such obstructions.

Their first checkpoint was Grand Marais, Michigan. The plan was to stop at Grand Marais for some breakfast and some gas.

The atlas showed the town just thirty miles down the lake. What the atlas didn't show was that the Grand Marais airport was built on a hill. Even though the clouds were still a few hundred feet above the water, the shore sloped up into the overcast. When the Cross Country fliers arrived at the town, the airport was completely obscured. So they continued on, enjoying the beauty of their shoreline a few hundred feet below.

By the time they got to Whitefish Bay—fifteen minutes later—it was clear that the weather wasn't getting any better. In fact, it seemed that the whole bay was enshrouded in mist—a solid wall between them and the eastern shore of Superior. Though the clouds over the lake were still several hundred feet above the water, the shore and everything inland was slowly being eaten by the fog.

It was obvious to Rick that there was only one thing to do. "Hey," he called, "I think we better turn around. The weather's looking pretty bad. We don't really have much choice but to head back."

Matt agreed.

John didn't. "What did you say?" he returned with a laugh. "For a second there I almost thought you said 'head back.'" He paused, then continued in a manner that welcomed no debate. "You know the rules. There's no turning back on the Cross Country. Besides, we only have another two weeks to get to Lubec, and we've got to reserve some down days for bad weather."

John swept his hand across what would have been the horizon on a clear day and pointed north over the lake toward the Canadian shore that lay twenty-five miles through the fog.

"The weather over the lake is fine," he continued. "I say we head straight for Canada. I bet the weather there will clear up a lot." It was a bet that came with some pretty high stakes.

"You can't just fly into Canada without a permit," argued Matt, thinking somehow that this technicality would have an effect on John's thinking.

It didn't. "You can if nobody asks for one," replied John with a grin. "We'll press straight along our path and land here." He held up the atlas and pointed to the Canadian town of Wawa. "Then we can follow Highway 101 all the way into Quebec. We can be in Maine by the end of the week. I say we give it a try. What's the worst that can happen?"

Before his passengers could provide the obvious answer to this question, John banked the Champ sharply to the left, diverting them north, around the worst of the weather and directly into the path of Dangerous Dave.

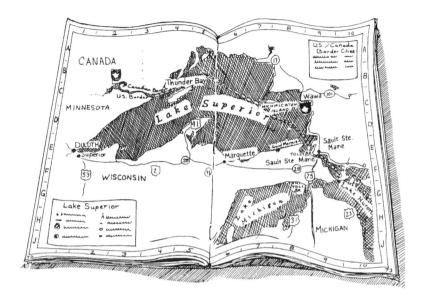

Within seconds of John's decision, all land disappeared. Rick knew that somewhere off to the east lay Saulte Ste. Marie and the locks that held back the waters of Superior and allowed ships to sail all the way from Duluth to ports throughout the world. But on that day he saw no ships, and the world had only a one-mile radius of visibility.

In the front John stared intently at the waves below, trying to maintain an attitude reference. In the back Rick and Matt exchanged frequent glances, trying to maintain their courage. They also looked occasionally at the small hunter's compass taped to the backseat. John also had a compass in front, but all the welding done on the Champ had magnetized its instrument cage to the point that any compass held anywhere near the instrument panel always read "E." This had been comforting when they had been going east, but now they were headed north. So they relied on the compass in the back seat to keep them from flying in circles.

* * *

A tense half hour later, when John spotted the Canadian shore-line through the fog, it seemed that his gamble had paid off. In fact, for a time it seemed that they would even be able to follow the road and leave the shore altogether. Right about the place where the road veered away from the lakeshore and left a good fifty miles of wilderness between itself and the water, they abandoned this plan. Although the weather had improved, the elevation had increased, and in places the land still rose to the clouds. John continued along the very relative safety of the shore.

Their feelings about this shore had changed during the day. Before Grand Marais they had commented to each other on how nice a particular beach looked for swimming. After Grand Marais they had commented on how a particular beach might be for landing if the weather got too bad to fly. Now the conversation centered on the question of whether they could survive if the engine quit and they had to ditch in the water next to the cliffs of this Canadian shore.

Their opinions varied on just exactly what to do if this happened. Rick thought it would be best to stall the Champ out in the water and try to get out before it sank. Matt thought it would be possible to put it into the water just offshore, drag the tail-wheel, and then pop the two main gear onto the narrow beach next to the cliff. John was willing to try either plan as long as he did the flying.

* * *

The weather didn't break at Wawa. Instead, it turned suddenly colder. Even though it was summer, it was beginning to snow.

Unfortunately, as at Grand Marais, the airport at Wawa was built on a hill. While the pilots could easily see the town below the clouds, the airport was hidden in the weather. John circled, trying to get a glimpse of the runway.

As time slipped by, Rick's eyes shifted to the Champ's gas gauge. It had something in common with the compass: It, too, read "E."

Rick looked to his watch. Factoring in the Champ's reserve fuel tank, he figured they had only about an hour of flying time left. They might be able to make it down to Saulte Ste. Marie if they turned back and followed the shoreline they had just covered. They certainly wouldn't if they waited much longer.

Rick was just bringing up the point that the "running out of gas" rule outweighed the "not turning back" rule when something out the side of the airplane grabbed Matt's attention.

"John," Matt directed, "bank a little back to the left." John complied, peering intently over his left shoulder. There, just barely visible through the snow, was an opening in the forest. It looked sort of like a runway.

"I think I see it!" Rick shouted, forgetting his fuel worries. "I don't know if you can make it, though."

"Yeah," returned John, "I can make it."

Rick grabbed a little tighter to the side of the seat, shot a worried look at Matt, but said nothing.

Committing himself to the landing without a whole lot of thought, no backup plan, and not a breath of a call on their hand-held radio, John headed for the opening. The closer they got to where they thought they had seen the runway, the lower John had to fly to stay out of the clouds. Finally they were skimming just a few feet above the trees. Rick held on, hoping the clearing they had seen wasn't just a parking lot, or at least not a small one.

Just when Rick thought they were goners, the Champ punched through a cloud and he saw the lights of a newly paved runway. He also saw the tops of two enormous pine trees sticking straight up in front of them.

With a yelp, John jammed the stick all the way to the right with both hands and at the same time stomped on the left rudder. The Champ swung into ninety degrees of bank, but the rudder kept it from turning into the trees. Out of the window Rick could see the right wing brushing though the thin branches of the small bushes a few feet above the ground.

In an instant they were through the trees. John reversed the controls, leveled the wings, and eased back on the stick slightly to catch the proper glidepath. The Champ passed just inches over the trees on the approach end of the runway and dropped softly onto the pavement.

"See," said John in a wavering tone, "I told you I could make it."

Matt and Rick, still recovering from the low-level aerobatics of the landing, were slow to answer. When they finally did, their words formed a mix between a prayer of thanksgiving and a curse on John for putting them through such a scare. But they had to admit, he had made it.

* * *

As they taxied through the snow and fog to a small brick building that appeared to belong to the airport's operator, a middle-aged woman wearing jeans and a heavy jacket embroidered with the words *Air Canada* came out to park them. They followed her signals to pull up next to a small green airplane the likes of which they had never seen. Constructed of steel tube and fabric, it was half the length of the Champ, with short wings mounted in the middle of the fuselage. A large bubble canopy dwarfed a very small tail. On the whole it looked like a loose confederation of bicycle and auto parts that had somehow been coaxed into taking to the air.

After John shut off the motor and they clambered out the door, the "Air Canada" woman approached the Champ. Rick expected to be interrogated about their illegal entry into Canada. The woman had other questions on her mind.

"Where did you guys come from?" she demanded. "I was sitting in the office listening to the radio and all I heard was the one airplane coming in from the north."

John looked at her without blinking. "Well, we just came in from the south."

The woman turned to look at the pilot emerging from the little green airplane: "You were the guy I talked to on the radio who just came in from the north, right?"

"Yeah," the man replied, "I guess so. And you were right about the weather moving in from the south."

"These guys just landed from the south," the woman said.

"How come I didn't hear you on the radio?" the man asked.

"Ahh, we don't have one," replied John, thinking fast.

Rick expected the man to be angry that they had nearly met him head to head on a runway in a snowstorm without making a radio call. Instead, the idea of another airplane coming in like that without a radio seemed to amuse him.

"Well, that was pretty gutsy flying coming in that way," was all he said.

"What do you mean gutsy?" asked Matt.

The man looked up from his work of tying down his airplane. "I mean coming in from the south what with the powerlines and all."

"What powerlines?" asked Rick.

"There's a huge set of powerlines blocking the approach from the south."

The truth dawned on each member of the Champ crew. They had flown *under* the powerlines!

"You mean you didn't know that?" the lone pilot asked. "You can see the powerlines on the charts."

John was quick to reply. "We don't have charts."

"How do you navigate?"

"With an atlas," replied John.

The man just laughed.

The woman shook her head as if they were all crazy and returned to the shelter of her office.

* * *

As the Champ fliers stashed their gear and brushed the snow from their heads, the pilot of the little green airplane asked them the familiar question about their craft. "What is it anyway?"

John answered in the usual way, but drew an unusual response. "That's great," the pilot said. "A three-place Champ with Stinson gear and tractor seats? And I thought my airplane was weird."

"It is," said John. "It looks more like a go-kart than an airplane."

"Yeah, it's a racer. I built it myself—"

John let out a breath of admiration. The man had built the airplane himself. This could mean only one thing: The little green airplane was a representative of something he held in great esteem—experimental airplanes. Ace's Champ was as experimental an aircraft as he had ever flown. But from magazines, he knew of a whole world of homemade death-defying, anti-gravity machines powered by everything from chainsaw engines to Ford V-8s. Subjected to only limited government supervision, the experimental aircraft was the last great bastion of the American dream.

That this man had fashioned his own niche in this dream was the kind of base upon which John could build a friendship. He extended his hand. The man shook it, then introduced himself. His name was Dave Allen.

Pleasantries complete, Dave continued describing his airplane. "It isn't quite perfect yet, but I've got it going nearly two hundred miles an hour. And even at that speed the Volkswagen engine is only burning about four gallons an hour. I've been trying to tweak it to set the Circum-Superior speed record for its class. I left home this morning thinking I could make the trip today but the weather started looking bad to the south so I decided to stop here. How about you guys, where are you headed?"

John related the saga-in-progress of the Cross Country.

"Guess that explains the atlas," Dave said after John had finished. "I used to do some of that kind of flying myself. One time I was going to visit a friend in Detroit. I got caught in some weather. Instead of landing or going back I decided to head straight across Lake Michigan—you can't hit anything over the water, right? Well, I got to the other side and had no idea where I was. Finally I found a sand beach to land on. It was a lot softer than it looked and I bent up the propeller pretty good. I borrowed a two-by-four and a C-clamp and got the prop straightened out, but it was still a pretty bad experience. But I don't suppose anybody who could make the approach you guys did would do anything stupid like that, huh?"

The Champ pilots looked at each other but said nothing.

Dave continued. "But hey—fifty bucks, a Vise Grip, and an atlas. That's a pretty good test, all right. I'll have to bring it up at the squadron when I get back home."

"What do you mean—squadron?" asked Matt.

"The 179th Fighter Squadron back in Duluth," replied Dave. "That's where I live. I fly F-4s there for the Guard."

Duluth? Rick's hometown? That sealed the friendship for Rick. And F-4s? An honest-to-goodness Fighter Pilot? That sealed the friendship for Matt.

* * *

The four men spent the evening kindling their new friendship by the light of a roaring fire at the Wawa lodge. Dave's room at the lodge cost him sixty dollars—outside the budget and the rules of the Cross Country. The fire, however, was free.

Outside, the snow-turned-rain poured down upon the land. Inside, the stories of Dave Allen played upon the imaginations of the Champ crew. This Dave Allen seemed to be a completely different man than the one who had just flown the Volkswagen-powered aircraft into Wawa in a snowstorm. This was Dave Allen, Fighter Pilot, and his tales of supersonic jets, enemy intercepts, and aerial duels mesmerized the young pilots. Here was a man who lived a life they could barely imagine—flying for the military in a way they had never dreamed possible.

Dave was a Guard Bum. He didn't have a house, and he didn't have a job, yet he was neither homeless nor unemployed. He lived in a hangar at the Duluth airport. He supported himself by sitting Alert for the Air National Guard, supplementing that income by developing experimental airplanes.

Despite the tenuous cash flow from his aircraft business, Dave refused to take on a normal job *downtown* and wouldn't consider flying for any airline that didn't charter single-seat fighters. Self-described as one of the best stick men in the country, Dave held a Ph.D. in Air Defense Alert. He was a full-time warrior on part-time pay, a true expert in combat tactics, undisputed champion of Air Guard pay extraction, and a bit of a loose cannon. To the three Champ pilots, he was a hero.

Before they met Dave, none of them had any idea of what the Air National Guard was about. Growing up, Rick hadn't even known there was a squadron in Duluth. The mental picture he had of the Guard was of a weekend flying club where old Air Force pilots were put out to pasture.

"That's not true at all," Dave explained as the night wore on. "I started out in the Guard. Learning to fly that way is the best kept secret in the country. We go to the same training, get the same commission, and fly the same jets as the Air Force. Heck, the Air National Guard *is* the Air Force, with a little different mission and philosophy. But there's one huge difference: As a pilot in the Guard, when you aren't flying, you don't have

any other duties. All you have to do is fly. Of course, you aren't
getting paid when you're not flying, but you aren't working
either."

This sentence burned deeply into Matt's mind. If there was
any one set of words he wanted to describe his life, this was it.
Because if flying was his work, then there really was no work at
all.

What lodged in Rick's mind was just one word, unspoken
thus far: freedom. "Let me get this straight," he said. "You're
telling me that if I can get in the Air Guard, they'll send me to
training and pay me to fly state-of-the-art jets just like in the Air
Force; but when I'm not flying I can design airplanes or build
bridges or whatever I want?"

"That's right," said Dave. "But here's the best part. When
you join the Guard, you join a specific unit. It's almost always
one near to where you grew up—that's just the way the Guard
works. Anyway, when you get through with training you're guar-
anteed to go back to that unit and fly the airplane the unit flies.
In the Air Force, you just join up and take what you're assigned.
In the Guard, you know from day one what you'll be flying and
where you'll be living, provided you have all the qualifications
and make it through the training.

"I'm from Minnesota and I wanted to fly fighters, so I joined
the 179th Fighter Squadron in Duluth to fly Air Defense. We sit
Alert kind of like the fire department. When an unidentified
aircraft comes into our ADIZ—that's the Air Defense Identification Zone—we go out and take care of it."

John had been listening intently. He couldn't take it anymore. He focused on his two gas stooge protégés. "You guys
have to do it. You have to give it a shot."

"I can't join the Guard just like that," Rick said. "Neither can
Matt. We've got to get jobs. That's what we've been working for."

John would have none of it. "Listen to yourself," he said.
"The whole time you've been in college you've been flying.

What are your best memories? Flying. What's the one thing you really like to do? Fly. You're a pilot."

Dave jumped in. "Listen, you guys. Almost everybody out there lives their lives in regret. They grow old by the mailbox waiting for the letter that's going to change their lives. If you're waiting for the letter saying, 'Please come to pilot training because your country needs you to fly fighters,' you're going to be waiting a long, long time."

Matt laughed. "Dave's right. It sounds like we just walked into the chance to fly the greatest airplanes in the world. It must have been fate that brought us here."

"The Champ brought us here," answered Rick.

"Exactly," returned Matt. "That's what I'm saying. You think the *Champ* is fun? Imagine flying a fighter. Maybe we'll make it, and maybe we won't, but at least if we try, we'll never have to stare up at the sky wondering."

Dave closed the sale.

"I know a few guys that might be able to help Matt here get in with the Air Defense unit in Vermont." He turned to Rick. "If you want to fly fighters for us in Duluth, I'll talk to my unit and see about getting you in." He handed Rick and Matt business cards as he continued.

"There's nothing greater than flying Air Defense for your country, especially right out of your hometown. You get to fly the best jets ever made—in defense of American soil. That's the Guard's responsibility. There's nobody else doing it, just the Guard. The original Minutemen; the militia putting away the forge and the plow to take up arms. The Guard is a tradition older than the country itself. It's citizen-soldiers fighting not for political theory, but to protect their land and way of life. And you know what pilot training is? It's the great equalizer. It's purely a question of ability. No money can buy it. No right of birth can guarantee it. It's not your family or your past; it's just you."

Rick shook his head. "You ought to be on a poster or something."

John jumped back in. "Look," he said, "all my life people have been telling me that flying a fighter is the greatest thing in the world. All I've ever wanted is to find out for myself. But they won't let me. They'll let you. Don't close a door that can never be opened again. You need to grab the brass ring now."

Rick nodded. "Okay, okay," he said, "I'll think about it."

And he did. All the way back on their walk to the airport, and long into the night after they had crawled inside the Champ's cockpit and thrown their sleeping bags over their bodies. He thought and thought and thought, until his thoughts gave way to sleep. Lulled into unconsciousness by the sound of rain splattering against the fabric above their heads, he slept, dreaming childhood dreams of little green airplanes, letters that never come, and fighters that were real, real fast.

* * *

Early the next morning Rick awoke to find his legs still asleep and his mind still filled with thoughts of fighters. He wasn't sure he'd ever walk again, but he needed to find Dave, so he cracked the door open and hoisted himself out of the Champ.

Looking about as he stretched his aching limbs in preparation for his walk into town, Rick saw that the clouds were gone. So was Dave's airplane.

Searching runway and ramp for the experimental craft, Rick found instead the ruddy face of the airport manager poking out of her office door. He hurried toward her.

Before he got there, the scream of a Volkswagen engine revved to full power cracked through the air. Rick changed course and rushed back to the runway. There, just lifting off, was Dave's little green racer. Rick raised his hand in a wave.

In reply, the aircraft rocked its wings, then pulled straight up, over the powerlines, and into the blue.

Oh, Rick thought, what I wouldn't give to be able to fly like that. Then he smiled. He knew what he would do.

CHAPTER IV

The Guard

Before acting, deliberate.
And when you have deliberated, act speedily.

— Martin Luther

DURING THE COURSE OF THE NEXT YEAR, Rick not only graduated from college, but, under the guidance of Dave Allen and John Macatee and with the zeal of the newly converted, took the multitude of tests, made the hundreds of phone calls, and filled out the mountains of security clearance forms required to complete his application to fly for the Duluth unit of the Air National Guard.

Everything went well. Four years of engineering classes had readied him for the mechanical reasoning, gauge reading, mathematics, and general-knowledge questions asked on the Air Force Officers Qualifying Test. A dozen years of video games had trained him for the computer-generated hand-eye coordination drill of the Basic Aptitude Test. Twenty-one years of good, decent Midwest upbringing made for a relatively clean security check.

Not all of the testing was easy. Had it not been for John, the psychological evaluation that asked Rick if he would rather (a) build an airplane or (b) plant a garden would have been quite a challenge. But John, having been through it all before, had told Rick to remember that although the evaluation used the word "would," what it really meant was "should." Looking at it like that, it was clear to Rick that if he wanted to be a fighter pilot, he "should" rather drive a race car than dance in a mime troupe.

Rick went into the physical examination, too, with a few of John's cards up his sleeve. He didn't need to use them on the electrocardiogram, the blood test, the hearing test or the hernia exam. He didn't need to use them on the dental exam—he had the required three natural teeth.

When he got to the eye exam, however, Rick was glad to have some bits of John's wisdom at his disposal. He knew that the allowable thickness of his glasses was directly proportional to the amount of money the Air Force had invested in his training. For him at that point, this was about a buck fifty—the price of the paperwork he had generated—so he needed vision, and eyes, that were without flaw.

When Rick entered the examination room at the Duluth Air Guard's clinic, the flight surgeon was the first to speak. "According to this chart you did quite well on all your tests so far. Twenty-fifteen. Twenty-seventeen. Not bad. But today's modern fighters require pilots with better than average eyes. Eyes are my business and it's my job to make sure that you have them."

Rick had no idea what the doctor meant by this, but whatever it was, it didn't sound good.

"So," the doctor continued, "we still have to see that there's nothing wrong inside your eyes. These drops will open them up so I can make sure everything is okay."

In went the drops and out went the doctor.

As Rick waited for the doctor's return he rested his attention on an eye chart pinned to the wall. He couldn't make it out. It was one giant blur. Rick turned his head to look around the room. Everything was a blur!

"I think you should be just about ready," the doctor said cheerlessly as he returned to take his place beside Rick.

Seemingly unaware of his examinee's quickened pulse, the doctor swung a large frame of lenses in front of Rick's eyes.

"Rick," he directed, "I'm going to change these lenses around, and I want you to look at the chart on the far wall and tell me if the blurring gets better or worse."

"What blurring?" Rick exclaimed, by this time terrified that there was something horribly wrong with his eyes. No amount of squinting could bring things into focus.

"You mean your eyes aren't blurred?" the doctor asked. "Those drops I gave you dilated your eyes and should have made it impossible for you to focus at all without these lenses. That is, if your eyes are normal."

"Ahh," Rick recovered. "What I meant was what *terrible* blurring."

The doctor eyed him skeptically. "Just tell me if the blurring gets better or worse."

Everything was a blur to Rick. Better, worse, worse, better—it all looked the same: horrible. Rick started to sweat. Profusely. He couldn't fail. He was going to be a fighter pilot. He had to succeed. So he mustered every eye muscle he had. He squinted and strained—and got nearly every answer wrong.

The doctor rolled his eyes in frustration. "Rick," he said, "what's wrong here? Don't you understand? I need you to tell me when it is more blurry or less blurry. The answers you're giving aren't making any sense."

It was then that Rick pulled out the ace John had put up his sleeve for just such an occasion. "If all else fails," John had told him, "try to confuse the doctors into helping you. They'll work with you. You just have to make 'em."

Rick hadn't understood these directions at the time, but now he did. Rick was already confused. All he had to do was bring the doctor into the same state.

"Oh," Rick said, "I thought you said you wanted me to tell you if the blurring was better or worse. Is more blurry better or is more blurry worse? I mean, blurry seems bad, but you said blurry is normal. I'm sorry, Doctor, I must be confused. Let's try it again. Maybe if you tried talking me through it a little."

"Okay, Rick," the doctor said, now noticeably impatient. "Let's try it one more time. Is it better now than before? It's better, isn't it Rick? Now it's less blurry, isn't it? Is it less blurry Rick?"

"Yes."

"Good."

It was happening! The doctor was working with him, just as John had said. Everything was looking good. Right up until the doctor left the room. Stepping out, he told Rick there was one little thing he needed to check.

One little thing! thought Rick. John failed his examination for one little thing! Rick slumped back in his chair, resigned to hear the worst.

After several minutes, or perhaps it was hours, the doctor returned. "Well, Rick," he said, "good news. You have a slight refractive error in your left eye, but it is within limits." A wave of relief swept over him. Another hurdle cleared.

* * *

Twelve months after Wawa and twelve days after his flight physical, Rick was back at the Guard base in Duluth, standing in front of a heavy wooden door with a brass sign bearing the words *Lieutenant Colonel David Johnson*. This was the big day for Rick. He had passed all the tests so far; on most he had done exceptionally well. But none of that mattered very much if this man didn't approve of him. Because as its commander, Colonel Johnson had the final say on whom the squadron sent to pilot training. And whom it didn't.

The door was ajar, and through the opening Rick could see a small desk completely covered with papers, books, and file folders. Colonel Johnson wasn't in.

As he waited outside the door, Rick felt increasingly self-conscious around the uniformed people who passed him in the hallway. He hadn't had a clue about how to dress for an interview for a job as a fighter pilot. Maybe he should have worn a suit and tie.

He hadn't even brought a briefcase. And what if Colonel Johnson wanted to conduct the interview over lunch? The colonel would ask him to drive, of course, as some kind of subtle fighter pilot test. If that happened, should he drive real fast and crazy-like, or would Colonel Johnson be looking for calm assurance in the driving of a potential fighter pilot? Standing there in the hall, mulling these things over in his tan pants and button-down shirt, Rick's confidence was tested by the certainty that he was both underdressed and unprepared to drive to lunch.

Rick's worry evaporated at the sight of a stocky, middle-aged man approaching the colonel's office. The man wore blue thermal underwear, a ratty old pair of gray gym shorts and Sorel winter boots. His ensemble was complete with a stocking cap bearing the logo of the Cloquet Lumberjacks high school hockey team. Trailing him closely were two children—a boy of about seven and a girl a year or two older. Both wore miniature shin-pads, boots, and hockey jerseys. Another northern Minnesota summer hockey season.

Rick tried not to stare as the three strode past him, continued several paces down the hall, and walked into Colonel Johnson's office. Rick followed and peeked through the door. The man had seated himself at the disheveled desk and was looking through the papers. The two children had picked up a pair of model F-4 Phantoms and were playing with them by the window overlooking a rain-soaked flightline of real F-4s.

Rick knocked twice on the half-open door. "Excuse me," he said, "I'm looking for Colonel Johnson."

The short man in the long johns looked up from his work. "Well, then," he replied, "you must have come to the right place.

I'm Dave Johnson." He waved a hand at the two children who
were now engaged in a full-up aerial battle. "These are my kids,
Bill and Nancy. You must be Rick Wedan."

* * *

The interview wasn't at all what Rick had expected or feared.
Colonel Johnson asked him how he had met Dave. Rick told
him about the Cross Country, hitting just the main points, high-
lighting the hours they had logged and the triumphant arrival
they had made in Maine, leaving out all mention of scud-running, Wawa, or siphoning gas out of unlocked truck tanks. They
were the stories that best described the trip, of course, but Rick
didn't think relating them would help his chances for flying
fighters.

Other than that, it was as if Colonel Johnson had no questions but had already made up his mind. He had just one issue
to get straight.

"Rick," he said, "this is not a game we play here. It is dangerous business, and we take it seriously. You want to fly fighters for us, and based on your background, your résumé, your
test scores, and Captain Allen's very strong recommendation,
we want you here."

Colonel Johnson cleared his throat.

"Flying a fighter is the most exciting thing you'll ever have
the chance to do, but you need to realize that for you to succeed is going to take years of hard work and commitment. You
also need to realize that, should the need arise, we're going to
ask you to use your training to fight and maybe to kill. That's
what the military is about. Bottom line. These days there are a
whole lot of people out there trying to dress it up and pretend
that it's just some kind of corporation like IBM or Pillsbury.
It isn't."

Rick nodded at the words, though his thoughts were on the
fighters outside the window.

Colonel Johnson continued. "Right now we have two armed F-4s and four men sitting Alert a quarter mile from here across the ramp. True Cold Warriors up here in Duluth ready to fly any time, in any weather. That's what Air Defense is about. It's like a game of chicken. The other side sends up aircraft to test our borders—to test our readiness and our will. We intercept them and let them know they can't just come waltzing into our airspace.

"As an Air Defense squadron our job is to protect the United States and preserve our air sovereignty. For most of my career I helped defend against a Russian bomber and missile attack over the arctic. Well, we beat the Russians, for the time being, anyway. That's why we'll be coming off Alert here next year and setting up a detachment down in Florida after our conversion to F-16s. Down there we'll be going up against anything that threatens our borders from the south.

"As you know, the world out there is changing. The threat is changing. It's not going away; it's just less defined. Now the threat is the unknown. In some ways that makes it more dangerous.

"I know all this is pretty hard to grasp right now. Only a fool thinks he can understand combat when he hasn't been there. But someday you might be asked to go up and do some shooting, so you need to have thought it through right from the start." Colonel Johnson paused. "Have you?"

Just then, the airplane in young Bill's hand crashed to the floor. As Rick watched the toy jet shatter into pieces, he realized that he had never thought at all about flying in the way Colonel Johnson had just described. He had fallen in love with thoughts of the excitement and the thrill and even the hard work and the challenge. But he had never stopped to consider the weight of Colonel Johnson's bottom-line message. This would have been a good time to regroup and reconsider.

But the next words out of Rick's mouth were not words of consideration. They were words of affirmation.

"Yes, sir," he said, quickly acquiring this most important of military skills.

"Good. Then welcome to the squadron," replied Colonel Johnson. "I've got to get the kids off to hockey practice, but I'll walk you down to the recruiters to get your officer school paperwork going."

A high-voltage current shot through Rick as he thanked the commander. He was going to pilot training!

CHAPTER V

The Academy

No one would have doubted his ability to reign
Had he never been emperor.

— Tacitus, *The Histories*

Rɪᴄᴋ's ᴘᴀʀᴇɴᴛs ᴄᴀᴍᴇ to the Duluth airport to see him off on his way to officer school.

It was a ritual they had performed many times before. They had held his hand on his first day of school. They had waved good-bye as he boarded the bus for camp and his first nights away from home. They had been there when he pulled his car out of the driveway on his way to college. They had stood there watching their little kindergartner's taillights disappear down the street, knowing that—although Rick would return in the spring and probably for several more springs to come—when he did return, he would not be the same.

But Rick had never gone off to something like this. When the outbound leg of this journey ended and Rick stepped off the plane, he would not be greeted by beaming camp counselors or Freshman Orientation Guides in cheery red T-shirts. He would be met by the military and they would take him away. At least that was what his parents thought.

* * *

Saddled with the nearly eighty pounds of dress blue uniforms, boots, fatigues, socks, shoes, towels, and other gear he would be needing for the six-week course at the Air Guard's Academy of Military Science (AMS), Rick looked around the Knoxville airport for the screaming drill sergeants he expected would whisk him off to training. He saw no one. So, after waiting for what he thought to be the appropriate time, Rick shouldered his heavy bags as best he could and stepped through the sliding doors to flag down a cab.

When the yellow taxi pulled to the curb, the driver jumped out to help Rick with his bags.

"Three bucks to AMS," the driver told him.

"What makes you think I'm going to AMS?" Rick asked.

The driver pointed to the green military suitcases stacked next to the young guy with the polished shoes and the short hair. "You don't have to be a brain surgeon," he said.

At the base security gate, the guard waved the cab through with a smile. They passed through the gate and continued on to park in front of a long two-story building. Rick got out, paid the driver the three bucks, loaded his bags onto his shoulders, and walked slowly toward half a dozen people grilling steaks on a small barbecue. The people waved to Rick, then directed him toward the front door of the building. So far officer school wasn't at all what his Hollywood-filled imagination had been expecting.

Just inside the swinging glass door, among an assortment of flyers and fire drill procedures, Rick found a list of names matched up to room numbers and flights. Scanning the names, Rick came to his own: "Officer Candidate Wedan, Richard W., F-16, Minnesota ANG." Next to his name, he saw the words "Room 106, C-flight." Across from the room number was his roommate's name, "Officer Candidate Thielman, Gregory G., F-16, Montana ANG." Rick noted the number and worked his way down the shabbily carpeted hallway until he found the room.

The door was open. Inside, a collection of underwear, T-shirts and fatigues was heaped on one of the two twin-sized beds. Four cans of Copenhagen and a pair of worn cowboy boots rested on the long desk built into the wall. Two large closets flanked the desk. Several pictures illustrating great National Guard battles hung on the walls. But by far the most noteworthy item in the room was the tall, lanky, unshaven man occupying the Naugahyde study chair, his feet propped up on the air conditioner, his right hand wrapped around a bottle of beer: Officer Candidate Thielman, Gregory G.

Like Rick, Greg was at AMS to earn his commission on his way to pilot training. Unlike Rick, Greg hadn't come to Knoxville by way of commercial airliner. He had driven the 1972 Ford pick-up his father had bought new for $4,000. The truck had a CB with a public address system, a toolbox, and a newly rebuilt engine.

It was this truck's original owner that had gotten Greg into the Guard. Even bigger than his son, Gale Thielman was a life-long guardsman, a chief master sergeant in the Montana unit and head of maintenance there. He was also the man who had taught Greg to properly spit his tobacco, which is what Greg did a second after saying "howdy" to Rick as he and his gear passed awkwardly through the door.

"Hi," replied Rick.

"You must be Rick Weedan, F-16 from Minnesota."

"Yeah, that's me, but it's Wedan, like sedan."

"Well, Wuh-dann, put your gear down. Looks like from this here book that we've got a little bit of work to do tonight," Greg said, motioning to a blue three-ring binder.

Rick dropped his bags and grabbed a seat on one of the beds.

"This ain't quite like Basic Training was, huh?" Greg asked.

"I don't know," Rick replied. "I've never been to Basic Training. I just swore in a couple months ago and have been waiting to come here to AMS."

"You're not prior-service?" Greg asked.

"Well, I've never been in the military before, if that's what you mean. Have you?"

Greg laughed. "Hell, yes. I've been in since God's dog was a pup. I was a crew chief on the F-106 for four years before I started turnin' wrenches on the F-16 when we converted two years ago. Best maintenance outfit in the world, the Guard. We've got more experience in just my family than the Air Force has in whole squadrons. My dad's been working on jets back home for thirty years. That's where he met my mom. Most everybody in my family has been in the Guard doing one thing or another. Nobody's ever been an officer, though."

Greg reached into his pocket, pulled out a shiny silver dollar and showed it to Rick.

"See this?" he asked. "My uncle got it for me to give to the first enlisted person to salute me after I get commissioned. He's the one who told me I had to be a pilot. He said I owed it to the Thielmans to go out and do some fighting in the airplanes the family has been working on for so many years. So I've been going to college part-time to get my degree. I finished that up and finally got a pilot slot. I thought that most of the people here were like me and had been in for awhile."

Rick hadn't known Greg long, but he already could guess that, prior-service or not, most people at AMS were nothing like his roommate.

Rick barely had time to come to this conclusion, however, when Greg spoke again. "So how did you get in? Do you have a lot of flying experience or something?"

Rick couldn't hold back. "Hell, yes, I've been flying since God's dog was a pup. Never flown in the military before, though."

Greg shook his head, spit expertly into a cup resting on the floor, then laughed. "Tell you what, then," he said. "Even though I know I'm gonna be a great pilot, since I don't have much actual flying time myself, how about we make a deal. I'll help you with the military stuff here and you help me with the flying stuff when we get to it."

"Do you think we'll be at pilot training together, too?" Rick asked.

"I'm sure of it," Greg replied. "When the Guard starts guys down a training track, like as not they'll be together the whole way. Especially if they're going to the same airplane."

"Well then," returned Rick, "you've got a deal."

"Good," said Greg, tossing Rick the three-ring binder. "Now start arranging your stuff."

And Rick did, following to the letter the book's directions on how to lay out every piece of clothing he had packed—from his five pairs of black socks to his two blue dress uniforms to his six pairs of Air Force issue drawers, *men's, brief length, white.*

"Since you missed Basic," Greg said as he directed Rick through the intricate directions of folding his underwear, "I'm going to let you fold some of my stuff tonight. I'm already pretty much of an expert. Folding underwear for inspections and making our beds were the two biggest parts of Basic."

"You've gotta be kidding," said Rick.

"No I ain't. Making the beds took twenty minutes a day. It had to be right. I remember one day when our instructor decided we needed more practice making our beds. So he comes and plays 'taps' on a tape recorder to make us all get under the covers. As soon as we're in he plays 'reveille.' We all jump out of our beds and start making them. As soon as we get done he plays taps and we have to get back into bed. Then he plays reveille again. Then taps. It went on for hours."

Rick shook his head in amazement as Greg continued. "The only thing more important than making beds was labeling and folding our clothes. We even got special Technical Orders—we call 'em T.O.s in the Air Force—specifying exactly how to do it."

"Kinda like this binder?" asked Rick.

"Same idea," answered Greg. "Every procedure in the Air Force—from arming nuclear missiles to changing engines—is spelled out in a T.O. They make all T.O.s follow the same basic format, so I guess they figure that if they write one for how to fold your underwear at Basic and you can follow it, then they can trust you to follow the steps to do just about anything."

"In any case," interjected Rick, "I guess that if you can't follow one to fold your underwear, you probably shouldn't be arming nuclear missiles."

"Now you're gettin' it."

Rick might have understood the concept, but he couldn't imagine that it was such a good screen. "Were there really guys that couldn't even fold their underwear?" he asked.

"There were guys that couldn't even pick out clothes," Greg replied. "I'll never forget this one Miernicki guy. On the day we were issued clothing, Miernicki was so nervous that he grabbed a pair of size fourteen boots. He was too scared to tell anyone they were too big, so he just laced them up as tight as he could and pressed on.

"For weeks we all wondered how anyone could be as unco-ordinated as Miernicki and still make it through life. Then we figured it out. It wasn't that he couldn't march; it was just that he was wearing boots that were five sizes too big!"

* * *

As Rick pulled an iron from one of his suitcases and got to work, Greg related more Basic Training pearls. "On one of our first days, our training instructor, Sergeant Gonzalez, had us sitting on the floor with our T.O.s open to the labeling page. He held up a hat for us.

"'This,' he said, 'is a hat. It has four parts. It has a front, a back, an inside and an outside. Do not write on the outside; write on the inside. Do not write on the back; write on the front. Write on the front inside.'"

"Talk about addressing the lowest common denominator," Rick said.

"Yeah," replied Greg, "but not low enough. Five minutes later, plain as day on the outside front of the poor guy's hat was the word *Miernicki*.

"The funniest thing was that Sergeant Gonzalez didn't say anything then. But for the next two weeks he asked us every day whether we had any problems with our clothing. Each time, Miernicki had to raise his hand and explain that he needed a new hat. Each time, Sergeant Gonzalez asked why, and Miernicki had to explain in front of the whole flight."

"That's pretty funny," Rick said as he filled the iron with more water, "but tell me—did Miernicki graduate?"

"Yep. It was amazing. Basic really turned his life around. After three weeks he started getting the hang of it. By the end of the course he could fold his underwear as well as anybody. Hell, he could even do a push-up. Come to think of it he ended up being a pretty good guy.

"Anyway," Greg concluded, "you can be glad this ain't Basic. If it was, you'd be spending two hours folding each T-shirt. You'd have to starch and press the entire shirt. Then you'd have to pluck and tweak the ends with tweezers until all edges aligned perfectly. If it didn't look like a brick, it wasn't ready."

Rick nodded in gratitude and noted that, two hours per shirt or not, it was already eleven o'clock and—since he was the only one folding—they weren't done yet.

When he mentioned this in hopes that Greg would pitch in and help, Greg came to a different conclusion. "Yeah, we'd better go to bed," he said.

Rick balked, saying they still had a lot to do.

"Look," Greg explained. "I've got a plan. At Basic you didn't have to think. They did it all for you. Here we have to decide what to do, when to go to bed, how much to sleep. I say the more we sleep the less time we'll actually be here doing stuff we don't want to do. If we sleep an extra hour a day for forty-five days, that's forty-five hours. A full work week that we're not here."

Greg had been a sergeant. Who was Rick to argue? So, while the rest of the dorm busied itself into the wee hours of the night, the occupants of Room 106 slept, preparing themselves efficiently for the days ahead.

For the next six weeks, in addition to ironing clothes, polishing shoes, and preparing for inspections, Rick and Greg filled their days learning the military knowledge they would require as officers. They heard military lectures, wrote military reports, gave military briefings, and took military tests.

Some of the most important lessons were learned outside the classroom. On the parade ground, they learned to steer squads of marchers gracefully with just a loud commanding voice. On the Leadership Training Obstacle Course they learned to organize themselves into units able to scale walls, ford rivers, and defeat hundreds of challenges, all with nothing but thirty feet of rope, three two-by-fours, and a rucksack.

The biggest leadership training tool at AMS was the daily operation of the squadron. The officer candidates themselves ran the school. There were student Wing Commanders, student Squadron Commanders, and student Flight Commanders.

Holding these positions was a bad deal. In addition to their normal officer candidate responsibilities, the student leaders had to look out for everyone below them. To do this successfully required a great deal of time. Therefore, holding such positions was woefully inconsistent with the Greg Thielman Strategy of Time Management.

For this reason, Greg sat down with Rick early-on to figure out a plan for staying out of these jobs. Drawing on his military gene-pool, he concocted a brilliant plan for staying out of the most difficult leadership jobs. The positions of authority, he said, were given to those people who needed the most training. He saw this right away because all the non-prior service people were given the jobs during the first week. Rick, for instance, was the C-flight resources officer responsible for making sure that, among other things, their bathrooms were always adequately supplied with toilet paper.

"If they think we want the jobs," Greg concluded, "they'll think we don't need the extra training. So what we need to do is *request* the leadership position."

Greg was the sergeant.

"Sir," Rick said to his instructors every chance he had during the six-week course, "I really think that I'm ready for a position of responsibility. I really enjoyed being C-flight resources officer, and I think I would make an excellent squadron commander."

To Rick's astonishment, the plan worked perfectly. Each week, while Greg and Rick stood in formation waiting to hear the names of the next week's commanders, they never heard their own. They never lost points for screwing up a command position, and they got more sleep than anyone in the history of AMS.

At the graduation banquet the night before they were to be commissioned, Greg's accomplishment was formally acknowledged. "Officer Candidate Thielman," the commander said into the microphone, "you have received the most honor points of anyone in your class. In fact, you received the least number of demerits of anyone in the past ten years. In addition, you have been singled out by your peers and instructors as an example of volunteerism and dedication. During your time here you have exemplified what it means to serve. For this accomplishment, I am proud to present you the General Gerald Ostern Award for Outstanding Achievement."

The commander then related the story of how General Ostern washed out of pilot training in the United States but joined the Royal Air Force in World War II to go on to shoot down five German planes. "This," the commander concluded, "is what we expect from an officer. This is what we expect of you."

It didn't seem to Rick like the type of performance that should be expected of them, especially right before pilot training. But Greg didn't seemed to notice. He just smiled for the camera and accepted the plaque.

* * *

The next day Greg and Rick received their golden second lieutenant bars. The last time Rick had seen the bars they had been on a board in the hands of the AMS commander. "These officer bars are yours for the taking," the commander had said. "They're not that much, all by themselves, but they're awfully heavy. They represent an officer's responsibility to uphold the Constitution and defend the nation. When you put them on, you'll bear that weight. You'll have to make the decisions. They won't always be clear cut, black and white. Sometimes you'll just have to make the call and live with the consequences."

Now, as his mother and father pinned the bars to his shoulders, Rick couldn't help wondering what decisions he would have to make during his career and what consequences his actions might have. Well, he'd find out soon enough, he guessed.

* * *

Immediately after the ceremony Rick watched as Greg stepped outside the auditorium and received a salute from an older Guardsman in a chief master sergeant's dress uniform.

The lanky young Montanan returned the salute then reached into his pocket for a certain silver dollar. He flipped the coin to his father—then shook his hand.

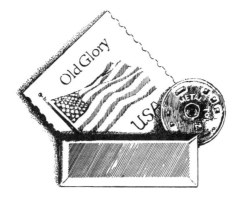

CHAPTER VI

FISHPOT

There are old pilots and there are bold pilots.
But there are no old, bold pilots.

— Adage of the Aviator

THREE WEEKS AFTER THEY walked across the stage at AMS, Rick and Greg arrived in San Antonio, Texas, for Flight Screening Program Officer Training. Because this name didn't make much sense, and because it could conveniently be abbreviated FSPOT, everybody called the place FISHPOT, which didn't make all that much sense either, but at least it was easy to say.

There were eighteen other students in their FISHPOT class. Four were from the Guard, three were from Air Force Reserve squadrons and nine were active duty Air Force.

The remaining two members of the class, Joao Paz and Cruz Dos Santos, were Portuguese students in the United States to be trained in the business of military flying. They had just finished up at the Defense Language Institute (DLI), also in San Antonio. At DLI, foreign students learned at least enough English to be able to speak safely on the radio. Those students who already spoke good English rode the DLI gravy train for six months while the rest of their class caught up enough to get through FISHPOT and then move on to flight school.

Immediately dubbed the Portu-guys, Paz and Cruz were virtual hoboes on the DLI gravy train. Speaking nearly flawless

English, the two had graduated with honors from the Portuguese Air Force Academy and had been given the coveted opportunity to learn to fly in the Unitcd States. If they won their wings in America, they said, they stood a good chance of being assigned to a fighter squadron back in Portugal.

* * *

The first day at FISHPOT, like the others to follow, began with a thirty-mile busride from Lackland Air Force Base, where the students lived, to the Hondo Municipal airport, where they flew. After they had situated themselves in a small classroom at the Hondo facility, the students were greeted by Captain Stephanie Padden, their academic instructor.

"Welcome to FISHPOT," she began. "I'm Captain Padden. For the next two days we'll be going over the fundamentals of the airplane you'll be flying here—the T-41 Mescalaro. It's really just a Cessna 172 with a few modifications. Some of you may already have flown 172s, but I guarantee you'll be flying them differently here.

"Those of you who make it past Flight Screening will be flying airplanes that are much more complicated than the Mighty Mescalaro, but the fundamentals you'll learn here will apply throughout your flying careers. So listen up. There will be a comprehensive test tomorrow afternoon." With that, Captain Padden launched into two days of non-stop aircraft academics.

"The first principle of flight you need to know," she told the class, "is that an airplane doesn't fly you. You fly the airplane. If ever you think the airplane is flying you, something's wrong. You've got to let the airplane know who's in charge. The second principle is that in the Air Force you don't fly to have fun. You fly to accomplish a mission. Here your mission is to prove you can learn to fly.

"Now then," she continued as she turned down the lights and turned on a slide projector, "an airplane has five main components: the fuselage, the wing, the empennage, the landing gear, and the engine…"

For the next two days, Rick, Greg, and the rest of the class were left to swim in a sea of aerodynamic theory and aircraft terminology. They learned about lift, drag, and thrust. They learned about rudders, ailerons, flaps, sticks, and throttles. They learned how they could use these controls to make a 1,500-pound machine take to the air.

"To control the flight of the aircraft," Captain Padden taught them, "you use the stick, the rudder, and the throttle. The stick controls the ailerons and the elevator. When you push forward on the stick, the elevator goes down. This causes lift on the tail to increase and forces the nose of the plane down. The opposite happens when you move the stick back."

Rick leaned over to Greg and whispered: "When you push forward on the stick, houses get bigger. When you pull back on the stick, houses get smaller."

Greg nodded in understanding as Captain Padden continued. "Side to side movement of the stick causes the ailerons, out at the edges of the airplane's wings, to move out of their streamlined position. When you move the stick to the left, the left aileron goes up and the right aileron goes down. This puts the airplane into a left bank. This is how airplanes turn. The lift from the wing pulls the plane around the circle.

"The rudder pedals," Captain Padden instructed, "are the other primary flight controls on the airplane. With them you control the rudder. Contrary to popular opinion, an airplane's rudder is not used for turning. It's used primarily to counteract adverse yaw, the undesired skidding of an airplane caused by unequal drag of the deflected ailerons. You can turn an airplane with the rudder, but then you skid, just like when you're in a car going fast around a turn."

* * *

Two days later, with their academic test behind them, Rick, Greg, and the others were led downstairs to meet their next challenge—their flying instructors. To everyone's surprise, these instructors were not Air Force pilots. They were civilians contracted by the Air Force to teach basic flying.

Having a civilian instructor was not something new to Rick. John was a civilian. Not being able to choose his civilian instructor, however, was something new. Of course, getting paid to fly was something new, as well, so Rick was ready to take the good with the bad.

As it turned out, there was no bad. Rick's instructor, Mr. Tex Wardlaw, was a wonderful teacher. Somewhere in his late fifties, Mr. Wardlaw had been an Air Force pilot and had retired after twenty years of flying transports all over the world. He had taken the job at FISHPOT both to supplement his retirement income and to pass on some of the wisdom he had gained in his years of flying. This was wisdom that Rick badly needed.

Immediately after they met their instructors, the students experienced their first official Air Force Flight Briefing. In the large classroom on the ground floor of the FISHPOT headquarters, Mr. Durkac, FISHPOT's chief pilot and flight examiner, briefed the students on that day's weather conditions, air traffic, and local hazards.

Then came something very new—the Morning Stand-Up Emergency Procedure (EP), a daily ritual that would torment the students throughout their flying training. By describing some terrible situation that might happen in the aircraft, and then immediately and without further warning "giving" the aircraft to some poor student to salvage in front of a couple dozen peers and instructors, the Air Force believed it could simulate the stress involved in actually bringing down an aircraft with a bent wing, hydraulic failure, or electrical fire. Of course, it was only a simulation. In the real aircraft, without all the people watching, there would be a lot less stress.

Rick was no stranger to aircraft emergencies. He was a Champ pilot. In the Champ, he had handled multitudes of emergencies. Most of these had required the same solution. When the engine quit, he landed. When the engine caught fire, he landed. When the rudder cable broke, he landed.

The Champ's systems were so simple that there really weren't many cockpit procedures that could remedy a problem, unless the problem was the result of doing something wrong in the cockpit in the first place—like forgetting to turn on the fuel valve.

In an Air Force jet, however, since there were lots of things that could go wrong, there were lots of actions the pilot could take to set them right. Though the T-41 was no jet and really was not much more complicated than the Champ, it was still an Air Force aircraft, so emergencies had to be handled the Air Force Way.

In general, the Air Force Way required running through the steps of the Air Force Emergency Checklist. In a time-critical emergency, however, such as engine failure on takeoff, there would be no time to refer to a written checklist. To handle these situations, the students learned, verbatim and by heart, a concise set of procedures typed out for them in boldface print. These were known as **BOLDFACE** procedures and every pilot of an Air Force aircraft, regardless of rank or status, was required to be able to recite and transcribe them without error.

For their first brief, the EP Mr. Durkac described was a blown tire on takeoff roll. It was really a very simple emergency. The procedure for handling it was right out of the study material Captain Padden had assigned the class the night before. But it didn't seem so simple what with everybody looking on. It was the first day of flying, after all, and the students were all terrified that they might be called on, get the Boldface wrong, and be grounded for the day.

So the entire class held its breath, working very hard to become invisible. Finally, after what seemed an interminable pause while he searched the room for the proper guinea pig, Mr. Durkac said, "Lieutenant Paz, you have the aircraft."

There were nineteen sighs of relief as the small Portuguese officer snapped smartly out of his seat and stood at attention. He said nothing.

"Lieutenant Paz," Mr. Durkac repeated, "you have just accelerated past fifty miles an hour and you hear a noise, feel the airplane settle slightly to the left and begin to veer off in that direction. You have the aircraft."

Rick could see the sweat starting to rise on Paz's Latin forehead. After an eternity, Paz spoke, in the worst English Rick had ever heard.

"Oh, sorry, sorry, I no cannot explain English."

As the American instructor excused the Portuguese student and looked around the room for another victim, Rick shook his head and smiled to himself at the cold brilliance of his foreign counterpart's plan. But he didn't smile for long.

"Lieutenant Wedan," Mr. Durkac said, catching Rick's subtle smirk, "you look like you might know how to handle this emergency. Maybe you can help Lieutenant Paz explain it in English for us. You have the aircraft."

Oh, brother, thought Rick as he jumped up and recited the Boldface for a blown tire, making a mental note to keep his eye on Paz and to keep his smirks to himself.

Rick's handling of the EP was not perfect, but it was good enough for Mr. Durkac—at least on that first day. The EP completed, the chief instructor dismissed the students into the care of their instructors and the beginning of their Air Force flying careers.

* * *

Given enough time, just about anyone could learn to fly the T-41. At FISHPOT, however, the students didn't just learn to fly the T-41; they learned to fly the T-41 in the Air Force. And they weren't given enough time; they were given three weeks.

The first two weeks were devoted to teaching the students to fly. At the end of that time, with only eight or nine rides under their belts, they were to solo the T-41 for a quick hop around the patch. Sometime during the third week they were to fly a ride with Mr. Durkac. Their performance on that flight would determine whether they had the flying aptitude required to be successful at Undergraduate Pilot Training (UPT). If Mr. Durkac felt they lacked that aptitude, he'd send them home—foiling their dreams, but saving the government a lot of jet fuel and a lot of money.

For a guy like Greg, with very little flying experience, three weeks wasn't much time to learn to apply the fundamentals of flight. The average first solo in the civilian world occurs when the pilot has logged fourteen hours. At FISHPOT Greg was expected to solo with only eight hours of flying time.

But Greg had two things going for him. First, he had Rick to tutor him. Second, he had no tainted flying past. His flying palette was clean; his hands and mind were like empty sponges ready to soak up proper skills and safe habits.

The same could not be said for Rick. Though John Macatee had taught him to handle an airplane in all sorts of hairy situations, he had never taught him to fly precisely to avoid those situations. To John, the more hazardous predicaments he put himself into and got himself out of, the better a pilot he was. The skill in his hands—his *stick power*—was all that mattered to John. Flying under bridges and powerlines and touching down on the sides of dams weren't dangerous stunts to be avoided, but displays of prowess to be lauded.

The Air Force had a different philosophy. As Captain Padden had taught in class, "a military pilot uses superior judgment to avoid situations requiring superior skill." Good hands were a prerequisite to wings, certainly, but they were not enough.

* * *

Rick's re-education included every phase of flight, from preflighting the aircraft to talking on the radio to entering the traffic pattern to land. Out at the hailsheds where the T-41s were stored, Mr. Wardlaw taught Rick to perform a complete preflight of the aircraft with direct reference to the preflight checklist. Having grown up flying the Champ—where preflight inspections were avoided for fear of finding something wrong that would ground the airplane—Rick found the lengthy and meticulous preflights to be a bit ridiculous. That is, until Mr. Wardlaw told him the story about the student who had gone up one day without checking the cockpit air vent intakes. The family of hornets that had decided to take up residence there hadn't been disturbed by the motor noise or the taxi out, but soon after lift-off the little fiends had come alive, swarmed into the cabin, and viciously attacked the student and instructor. Luckily, the two had been able to get the plane back on the ground and escape from the cockpit before being overcome by inflammation.

Mr. Wardlaw also taught Rick to sound like a professional on the radio. This was very important, for psychological as well as tactical reasons. A botched landing preceded by a strong, confident radio call would be written off by observers as the result of some unseen turbulence. A perfect landing preceded by a weak and stumbling radio call would more than likely be considered a fluke.

Rick's Champ training had done nothing for him in this respect. Though they had carried a handheld radio in the Champ, its transmission capability was very limited. In the receive mode, however, they could always clearly make out such calls as "Champ departing Palo Alto, it appears you're on fire." Because the radio received so well and because the Champ so often appeared to be on fire, after a while they had decided it was better to work exclusively out of Skysailing and stay away from places where they had to use a radio.

* * *

Not everyone using the runway at Hondo adhered to the strict radio protocol imposed by the Air Force. This was because the Air Force didn't own the airport; it just used it. There wasn't even an official control tower, just runway supervisory units for the T-41s. So, legally, anyone could just fly in and land. Not many civilians who valued their airplanes flew into FISHPOT during student training. But one man did. And did so consistently.

His name was Yancy, and he flew an old yellow Stearman cropduster. Yancy had learned to cropdust when pilots had to be kicked awake by flagmen and fueled with coffee as they emerged from their various states of drunkenness. Coming from this background, Yancy would often scoot in among the students with no radio and no fear.

In his big yellow biplane, Yancy represented the flying Rick had done in the Champ—the kind he needed to stay away from at FISHPOT. Yancy's aviation was seat-of-the-pants flying, with no instruments and no rules.

Flying in the military was a different thing altogether. As a military pilot, Rick was required to fly at certain airspeeds and certain altitudes and follow certain procedures. There was no room for making up rules when flying at 100 feet and 500 knots in an F-16. So there was no toleration for free-lance at Hondo when learning to fly at 1,000 feet and 100 knots in a T-41.

* * *

Rick's checkride drove this point home. In the assigned practice area defined by Highway 90, an old ranchhouse, and a large corral, Rick demonstrated that he could roll into sixty degrees of bank and maintain his airspeed and altitude.

After a series of practice stalls during which Rick pulled the power back and slowed the airplane until the wing just quit flying, he keyed the radio and said, "Stomp two one, area five, request return to base."

"Cleared Zulu recovery," the controller replied.

In accordance with procedure, Rick turned the airplane to the north and headed for Highway 90. At the highway, Rick banked to the right and followed the two-lane track east to the airport at exactly 3,100 feet and exactly 100 knots.

Entering the traffic pattern, Rick called the runway controller. "Stomp two one, right downwind."

"Roger, Stomp two one," the reply came. "No other traffic in the pattern at this time. Report base."

"Stomp two one."

As Rick approached the small mobile home he knew marked the spot where he needed to turn the base leg perpendicular to the runway, he reduced his airspeed to exactly 90 knots, put the flaps down 20 degrees, and made his turn.

If Rick had been flying the Champ, he would have flown over the field with no radio contact, taken a look at the windsock to see which way to land, and spiraled down or slipped the airplane to make the landing. There would have been no concern for airspeed or altitude control. In fact, the worse the approach, the more glory in salvaging it with a good landing. Wawa, for example, had been the worst approach and the greatest landing of all.

Turning to line himself up for final approach, Rick realized how different this was. He wasn't screaming in under unseen power lines. He was slowing to exactly 75 knots by pulling the power to exactly 1,800 rpm.

Just when Rick thought he had the airplane properly leveled and stabilized for a four-mile final approach, something
caught his eye out of the bottom left side of the canopy. He
turned his head. There, plain as day, was Yancy's big yellow
biplane skimming a few feet over the fields, a quarter of a mile
back and gaining fast.

It was clear to Rick what was going on. Yancy was trying to
beat them in. Because Yancy was lower than Rick, by regulation he would have the right-of-way if he could get at least even
with the T-41. The regulation also prohibited intentionally using altitude to get this advantage, but Rick didn't imagine that
part mattered too much to Yancy.

Such conduct from another pilot could not be tolerated. It
was a challenge that simply could not be ignored. Yancy's plane
was powerful, Rick knew, but the T-41 was faster. Rick was
going only 75 knots, but that was just a procedural speed. He
could easily raise the flaps, add some power and use their altitude to cut Yancy off.

If John Macatee had been in the airplane, he would have
had Rick push the power up to redline rpm and drop the nose
to gain airspeed. And then it would have been a race to the
airport—at fifty feet above the ground.

But it wasn't John Macatee sitting next to Rick. It was Mr.
Durkac, the FISHPOT flight examiner. And it wasn't a Champ
they were flying. It was a T-41. It was just a small propeller
airplane, but it belonged to the Air Force, and flying it meant
abiding by all the rules established for Air Force pilots. So, as
much as he hated to do so, Rick tapped Mr. Durkac on the arm
and pointed over his left shoulder to the biplane that was just
beginning to pass them by.

"Mr. Durkac," Rick said, "I see another airplane off to our
left. It looks like he's ahead of us. I'm going to execute the go-
around procedure." And this is exactly what Rick did, leveling

off and committing himself to flying around the pattern one more time. A hundred feet below, Yancy pulled ahead.

By the time Rick finally got on the ground and was taxiing by Yancy's cropdusting operation, the old-time pilot was already refueling his biplane—its engine still running—and refilling its tanks with pesticide.

Waving to Rick and the examiner as they taxied past, Yancy laughed and shook his head. Rick looked away to taxi the T-41 into the hailshed one last time. Yancy had won, all right, but as the T-41's four-cylinder piston engine drew its last breath, Rick savored a victory of his own. He had just bridged the gap between the civilian and the military worlds. FISHPOT was over, and the next airplane he would fly would be a *jet*.

CHAPTER VII

Del Rio by the Sea

The rivers run to the ocean,
Yet the ocean is not full.

— Indian Proverb

Rᴉᴄᴋ ᴍᴏᴠᴇᴅ ʜɪᴍsᴇʟꜰ ᴛᴏ Laughlin Air Force Base in Del Rio, Texas, for his year of Undergraduate Pilot Training (UPT). He got the scoop on the move from Colonel Johnson soon after returning home from FISHPOT. The commander himself had gone to Laughlin for training years before and told Rick just what to do to get there. "Throw your stuff in your car, head south for a couple days, and take a right. You can't miss Del Rio; it's right in the middle of nowhere."

Dave Allen had reinforced Colonel Johnson's directions. "Move your stuff yourself," Dave had advised. "If you let the government move your stuff, you might never get it. If you do it yourself they'll pay you eighty percent of what it would have cost the government to move your stuff. You can make some pretty good money, especially if you have some heavy stuff."

It sounded like reasonable advice to Rick, so he packed up all his belongings, crammed them into his station wagon, said good-bye to the cold of northern Minnesota, and turned south onto Interstate 35.

* * *

After two days on the road, Rick finally came to San Antonio, where he hooked right onto Highway 90 and headed west, toward Hondo and the remaining 150 miles to Del Rio.

Fifty miles out of San Antonio, Rick passed the last tree he would see until he got to Laughlin. Looking at the landscape around him, he had to laugh at the memory of the map that Colonel Johnson had shown him back in Duluth when he had told him that he was going to Laughlin for pilot training. The map had included all five pilot training bases in the country but had shown only the outline of the United States. On the map, Del Rio looked like a coastal town. Now Rick could see for himself what kind of a coastal town it was—one with a desert beach 200 miles wide.

Why exactly the Air Force had placed a pilot training base so far out in the desert would generate a great deal of discussion among the students at Laughlin during the year, but it wasn't a question that troubled Rick. He might be living in the desert, but he would be living there to learn to fly jets.

* * *

When Rick saw a sign reading "Del Rio—25 miles," he knew the dream lay just a few miles ahead on the long, straight highway. Just a few more minutes away in his low-riding station wagon.

Jets, he thought. *I wonder if I have what it takes to fly jets.* He didn't know what "it" was, or how to get it if he didn't already have it, but he was pretty sure it wasn't the same thing that had allowed him to pass the Air Force Officer Qualifying Test or to have done well at Officer School. It was probably closer to the skill required to land a beat-up old taildragger on a gravel road in California. At least he hoped it was.

One thing the second lieutenant was dead certain about, however, was that even though it was almost December, he was hot. His station wagon, a true Minnesota vehicle, had snow tires but no air conditioning. Rick wished it had. He also wished that he had put sunscreen on his left arm, which was turning a bright red from the desert sun beating down through the open window.

When over a hill a mile or two distant Rick saw the airborne silhouette of a T-38 Talon, these concerns and even the sweat on his forehead, it seemed, evaporated. Long and sleek, the T-38 streamed through the air like a white rocket. Rick nodded his head and allowed himself a big smile at the sight. That jet was the reason for his journey.

Would he really be able to fly an airplane like that? As an elementary school student, he had always frightened himself on the first day of class by looking at the end of his arithmetic book. The chapters on long division and fractions had petrified him. He couldn't do those things; he was going to fail third grade.

Over the years, though, he had learned to take challenges one step at a time. Yet here was the T-38, the end of the UPT book. And he couldn't take his eyes off it.

* * *

The next day Lieutenant Rick Wedan started Pilot Training. Air Force Pilot Training.

At Laughlin's front gate, flanked by towering palm trees, Rick joined a long line of cars waiting to get through. As he waited, he searched through the hamburger wrappers, coffee cups, and half-eaten bags of chips that littered the passenger seat of his car to find the letter telling him where to go.

It was addressed to students of class 92-01; that was his class. They were to be the first class to graduate in the fiscal year 1992. Rick scanned the letter. "Welcome to Laughlin and UPT," blah, blah, "one of the most challenging programs in the world," blah, blah, "hard work…well worth it in the end." Blah, blah, blah.

There at the bottom was the important stuff. "Report to the Squadron Operations Building at 0730 in Class-A Blues, cleanly shaven, with proper haircut and military appearance." Rick ran his hand over his face, wishing he had shaved more thoroughly, but glad he had remembered not to pack his uniforms beneath his weight set in the back of his wagon.

Arriving, finally, at the front of the line, Rick received a salute from the security guard who acknowledged the blue officer insignia on his front bumper. Rick saluted back as he debated whether to stop and ask for directions. Looking at his watch, Rick decided that he really didn't have time to stop, so he pushed down on the accelerator and pulled through the gate.

Twenty minutes later, Rick concluded his base tour with a stop at the backside of the same front gate. This time he got out of the car, walked up to the guard, and explained what he needed. The guard tried unsuccessfully to hide a smile and pointed down the road.

"You need to go down this road three blocks," he directed. "Take a right at Vance Street, then go two more blocks to Williams. Take a left there. You'll see the Squadron Building right next to the flightline. You can't miss it."

Although Rick had already proved the guard wrong on this point, he was in a bind for time, so he decided to take a chance and follow the guard's directions.

As he approached the rows of shiny white jets lined up in front of a group of buildings, Rick spotted the old Cadillac he knew belonged to the Portu-guys.

Parked next to the Cadillac was an aging brown-and-white Ford pickup with Montana plates. The truck had no topper, and its bed was filled to a good three feet over the level of the cab with an assortment of household goods. They were covered with a large green tarp and strapped down with yellow nylon rope. The truck's rear end was sagging so low it looked like it might drag on the ground at the slightest bump. Apparently his old AMS roommate had opted for the financial incentives of a do-it-yourself move as well.

Rick pulled his car into the empty spot next to the truck just as Greg stepped out of the cab with a bundle of papers in his hands.

"Hey, Greg," Rick called as he grabbed his own paperwork and jogged toward the truck. "Do you know where we're going?"

"Yeah," replied the Montana rancher, "I was just up there, but I forgot my Copenhagen in the truck." Greg ran a finger around his lips, then swallowed once. "We'd better hurry or we'll be late."

With this, Greg led Rick through a set of large double doors and up a flight of stairs to a room at the end of a long hallway.

Greg opened the door to the room and they stepped inside. Just as they took their seats at the back of the room, another door opened. In walked a captain in a well-worn flightsuit. The class came to attention.

The captain told them to take their seats, then said: "I'm Captain Steve Vautrain and it's my pleasure to welcome you to Undergraduate Pilot Training. I know this is the day you've all been dreaming about for years. Well, wake up. You're here. Pilot training. It's gonna be the best year of your lives.

"I've gotta warn you, though, it's gonna start out kind of slow. Today, and for the next week or so, we'll be doing in-processing and in-briefing. After you get your gear, you'll have two weeks of physiology class and systems academics. Then you'll hit the flightline. That's when UPT really begins. I'll be in charge of you until then. I'll also be teaching you your systems academics.

"For starters today, how about everybody handing me your paperwork so we can get that going. While I collect it, why don't you all go around the room and tell everybody who you are, where you're from, and where you were commissioned."

As the introductions began, Rick looked around the room at the thirty people with whom he would spend the next year of his life. He knew only four of them that first morning: Thielman, Paz, Cruz, and Emily Breuner, a friend from AMS who was preparing to fly C-141s for the Tennessee Air National Guard. Of the rest he knew nothing, though from the introductions he was learning enough superficialities to make baseless and faulty judgments about his classmates' personalities. He had no way of knowing, however, who would be good, who would be bad, and who would be dangerous. But then, that was what they were at Laughlin to find out.

The class had some diverse backgrounds. In addition to Greg, Rick, and Emily, there was one other Guard student: Bud Jones, a long, spindly captain who had been a Weapons Systems Operator in the backseat of the F-4. Bud would be flying the F-16 for the Massachusetts Air National Guard.

There was one other captain in the class—a former B-52 navigator named Buck Shawhan.

One student had a future job flying C-141s for the Air Force Reserve in Delaware. The others were all newly commissioned second lieutenants from the Air Force Academy and college Reserve Officer Training Corps (ROTC) programs. Some, like Karen Policano, a banner-towing pilot from New Jersey, had come to UPT with thousands of hours of civilian flying time. Others had come with only their FISHPOT experience.

When it came his turn to introduce himself, Rick recalled the story about Air Force introductions that Emily had related to him at AMS. Her brother was also in the Memphis unit and had gone to pilot training a few years earlier. Back when he was a student, his wife had gotten together with the wives of the other students. At that first meeting they had all told where they were from and what airplane their husbands hoped to get out of pilot training. The active duty wives had said things like, "My name is Sherri Bond, my husband is Darren, we're from Indiana, and Darren hopes to fly an F-15 and get stationed somewhere in the East." When Emily's brother's wife had spoken the message was different. "My name is Susie Breuner," she had said, "and my husband is Charlie. When he graduates, we're going to move back home to Memphis, and he's going to fly the C-141."

The wives had looked at her in shock. "What do you mean he's *going* to fly the C-141 and you're *going* to move back home to Memphis? You don't know that until assignment night."

"Oh," Susie had replied. "I guess you didn't know. Charlie is in the Guard."

Most active duty wives hadn't known exactly what it meant to be "in the Guard," her sister-in-law had told Emily, but they all had known enough to think to themselves: "What's wrong with my husband? How come he isn't in the Guard?"

Well, even though he knew it was probably not true, Rick had laughed pretty hard when Emily had told him this story. But that had been at AMS, an Air Guard school. Here at UPT he had no intention of setting himself apart. So, in his introduction he down-played his Guard connection the best he could. Unlike Greg.

"My name is Greg Thielman," he said as he stood up. "I'm in the Montana Air Guard. I've been in the Guard for seven years, and when I get out of here, I'm gonna be a fighter pilot back home right where I grew up."

Rick closed his eyes, shook his head, and wished that he had been sitting in a different row.

* * *

Following the introductions, the first morning dragged into the
first afternoon and the first day dragged into the first week.
There was no talk of flying, just talk about paperwork, orders,
household shipments, fire protection, and personal safety. After what seemed like a few hundred of these talks, it became
difficult to tell where one lecture ended and the next began.
They all sounded the same. One unit representative after another walked into the room and said things like, "Good morning, I'm Sergeant Matheson from the Laughlin Safety Office. I
don't know anything about ailerons or engines, but I do know
that if you put your toilet seat up too high your feet can fall
asleep, and that can be dangerous..."

What kept the students going was the schedule of daily
events they carried with them everywhere. The schedule told
them where to be, how to get there, and when they had an
hour or two of free time to get situated in their dorm rooms on
base.

The schedule also told them when they were to be issued
their equipment. When that day finally came, a week into the
program, it was like a birthday—only better. Because on that
day they didn't get birthday suits; they got flight suits. They
didn't get birthday gloves and jackets; they got flying gloves
and flying jackets. Instead of shirts, socks, and ties, they got
flashlights, flight computers, and custom-fit Air Force Kevlar
and graphite helmets.

As the class filed out of the helmet shop, Captain Vautrain
handed each of the students one final piece of equipment—the
silver-embossed black leather nametags they would fasten to
their flightsuits just over their hearts. But one feature was miss-
ing. Above their names was a void where their wings belonged.
They would spend the entire year trying to fill that empty space.

* * *

Wings or not, just having the UPT nametags meant the class members could finally wear their flightsuits and no longer had to wear their dress blues around base. Apart from being uncomfortable, the blues had set them apart as an underclass amongst the UPT citizens. When they walked around in blues, everyone knew they were the new class. The other classes were glad to know this because it meant they could cut one more notch in the countdown toward their own graduation. The happiest class of all was the one that was being replaced. Class 91-01 had been waiting a year to see Class 92-01.

The students needed one last accoutrement on their flightsuits to complete their integration into the pilot training mainstream. They needed a class patch on their left sleeve to complement the 57th Flying Training Squadron patch on their right.

After much deliberation, 92-01 decided on a design featuring a straight-out proclamation of how they felt about themselves and the year they would be spending in the desert. The patch was a black cowboy silhouette on a white background along with the lone-star flag of the state of Texas. No longer were they just class 92-01. Now they were the *Modern Day Cowboys.*

For the next two weeks, the newly anointed Cowboys donned their flightsuits each day and made their way to seven o'clock reports at the physiology building. There they learned the effects that flying jets would have on their bodies. They learned about spatial disorientation, g-induced loss of consciousness, and the perils of smoking before flying at night. They learned about the inner ear, the eustachian tube and the gastro-intestinal tract.

After learning in class how the low pressure of high altitude would make the gases in their body cavities expand, the class got to see the effects first-hand in the hypobaric chamber. An airtight steel box big enough to seat a dozen people, the chamber had a station for each occupant complete with a communication cord and an oxygen regulator. With their newly acquired helmets fit tightly to their heads, the students plugged themselves into these connections.

They began the training profile by breathing pure oxygen for thirty minutes. This reduced the amount of nitrogen in their blood and lessened the chance of the gas coming out of solution at altitude. After thirty minutes the instructors shut the airlock door and pumped the air out of the chamber to simulate ascent in an unpressurized airplane.

The instructors took the chamber up and up and up. At a simulated 25,000 feet they stopped the ascent and directed the students to remove their masks and breathe the ambient air in the chamber.

When it was his turn to drop his mask Rick realized immediately where all the expanding gases from within their bodies had gone. It was dangerous to try to hold these gases in, so the instructors had taken time to teach a variety of techniques to relieve the pressure quickly and efficiently. It hadn't been a test. However, based on the smell in the chamber, everyone in the class had passed.

The purpose of the chamber, though, was not to test the students' gag reflex. It was to demonstrate the danger of hypoxia—lack of oxygen in the blood. So that they could see the decline in their mental abilities when suffering from hypoxia, the students were given pads of paper and pencils and told to write their names ten times. A look at the completed paper at the end of the chamber ride was a good lesson to any student thinking it unimportant to wear an oxygen mask at high altitude. The first two lines, written during the first fifteen seconds at altitude were nearly perfect. The last two or three lines, written two minutes after removing their masks, were nearly illegible.

* * *

Aircraft egress was the final phase of physiology training for the Modern Day Cowboys. The class learned several ways to exit the T-37, the first jet they would be flying at UPT. The simplest and most dramatic was to raise the handgrips on the sides of their ejection seats and squeeze the triggers. This would jettison the canopy and fire the automatic, ballistic-powered seat. Ejecting was easy. The hard part was hitting the ground.

To prepare them for this impact, the physiology instructors subjected class 92-01 to the rigors of the gravel. First they made the students jump off towers into piles of gravel. Then they swung them by harnesses and dropped them into pits of gravel. Then they dragged them by parachute straps through fields of gravel to teach them how to release the harnesses after impact.

Provided they could still walk, the students completed their egress training by parasailing behind trucks. Five hundred feet below them was a field of Air Force gravel, carefully prepared to encourage the students to do whatever was necessary to make a soft landing.

* * *

Soon after passing through the rigors of parachute training, the Modern Day Cowboys began their first aircraft academics in preparation for the flightline. The first class on the syllabus was T-37 Systems, taught by Captain Vautrain.

"You're going to find," said Captain Vautrain on the first day of class, "that UPT uses the firehose approach. At first you will be overwhelmed with information, both here and when you get to the flightline. You will be thirsty for knowledge, but when you step up to drink you will find that you are drinking not from a fountain but from a firehose. Don't let that worry you. The T-37 is a simple jet."

Rick and his class knew that Captain Vautrain was right. The T-37 was a simple jet. It was simply old, simply slow, and was made by Cessna, just like the T-41. But the T-37 was a *jet*. And that, in and of itself, was overwhelming. And what was more, simple or not—they learned every single thing about it.

They learned that because its two J-69 turbofan non-afterburning engines made it sound amazingly like a three-ton dog whistle, the jet was called "The Tweet." They learned that, in addition to featuring large, straight wings, a high tail, and side-by-side seating, the Tweet's control surfaces were moved by conventional cable linkage. They learned that the jet was a good all-around trainer capable of speeds up to 250 knots.

They learned Tweet statistics, Tweet operational limits, and Tweet schematics. They learned the number of rings on the trim button. They learned what part of the T-37 was made of wood, what part was edible, and what part they could drink if they had to. They learned how to start the jet and what to do if they couldn't.

Most of this information came from formal sources: Air Force publications or prepared lectures. The most important publication was T.O. A-37-1, the Air Force technical order for the T-37. Known as the "Dash-1," this manual described the T-37 and how to fly it, much like the technical orders at Basic Training described underwear and how to fold it.

Other information was taught, as the saying went, in pilot terms. Captain Vautrain displayed this during his lecture on the Course Indicator, the principal navigation instrument in the T-37. After going over the textbook's explanation for the better part of an hour to a roomful of glassy eyes, a frustrated Captain Vautrain gave up on the textbook explanation and tried a new tack. "Look," he said, "here's how we used to do it when I was a student: When you're trying to get back to your area, dial in the center radial, then pretend that the Course Indicator needle is a toilet seat and you're sitting on it facing along the arrow. The toilet paper is always on the Course Deviation Indicator. To get back to your area you simply reach for the toilet paper and turn the jet in that direction. Just grab the toilet paper and you'll never go wrong..."

What the heck? Rick thought. Here they were, training to fly jets in the most advanced Air Force in the world, and they were being admonished to remember the toilet paper. It sounded more like advice for successful camping than for flying a jet. On the other hand, it did make sense.

* * *

There seemed to be a never-ending amount of material to learn. Forget Captain Vautrain's analogy, Rick thought. Studying at UPT was more like painting the Golden Gate Bridge than drinking from a firehose. By the time he finished going through one set of study material, he had already forgotten the beginning, so he needed to start all over again.

Through steadfast repetition, however, as the first academic portion of pilot training came to an end, Rick felt he was making headway. If nothing else, he had come to a clear understanding of when to grab the toilet paper and when to grab the emergency fuel shutoff handle. Maybe Rick wasn't ready to build a T-37, but by the time he took the T-37 Systems test he was certain he was ready to fly one.

He was wrong.

CHAPTER VIII

Morning Brief

I'd maintain aircraft control,
analyze the situation, take appropriate action,
and land as soon as conditions permit.

— Opening line of UPT Stand-up EP

During their weeks absorbing aviation academics, Rick and the rest of the Modern Day Cowboys observed some semblance of a normal work schedule. Though they put in twelve-hour days in the classroom, the days at least started at hours when there was traffic on the streets. Once they hit flightline, this schedule—and everything else—changed completely.

To make the most of the limited number of jets available, half of the classes reported at four or five in the morning while the other half came in at nine or ten. The prospect of waking in the wee morning hours didn't bother Rick. During college he had worked nights, one whole summer, at a Green Giant factory back in Minnesota. The only thing different about being in Texas was that, instead of getting up in the middle of the night to run corn cobs through cutters, he would be getting up to learn to fly jets.

What did bother Rick was that this schedule alternated. One week would be early week; the next would be late week. From his factory shiftwork experience, he knew that, if followed long enough, any schedule would become comfortable. A week was about the right amount of time to get used to a schedule. But because the UPT reports alternated weekly, this meant that just as he was adjusting to sleeping in until nine for a ten o'clock report he'd have to switch and start getting up at three in the morning to be in by four.

* * *

The first day on the flightline for the Modern Day Cowboys was Monday of an early week. It was early week for the entire squadron. Because it was the new baby class, 92-01 had the earliest report of all—0400.

In preparation for this early hour, Rick went to bed at seven on Sunday night. Falling victim to his circadian clock, however, he lay awake for hours in his dorm room with the shades pulled and the noise of the world outside filling his ears. Finally, he drifted off to a restless sleep, only to be shocked a few hours later by the blare of his cheap Air Force clock radio playing mariachi music just to remind him that he was still in Del Rio. Outside the window the world was pitch black. But he roused himself and started the coffee because he was a student at UPT and he was going to learn to fly jets.

* * *

Following the short pre-dawn drive from the dorms down to the flightline, Rick parked in the T-37 lot and made his way into the squadron building. Half a dozen of his classmates were already there when he arrived, and together they searched the building's quiet hallways until they found the flightroom for B-flight, the flight to which they had been assigned.

Stepping through the doorway into the room, Rick saw about him a single large open space with fifteen or so desks and twice as many chairs placed in an orderly fashion throughout. In the front of the room stood a podium and a blackboard. In one corner was a walk-around counter behind which hung several large magnetic scheduling boards. The walls of the room were covered with pictures of jets and previous B-flight classes.

Other than that, the room was empty and very quiet. Not a single Instructor Pilot (IP) was to be found. As on every morning to follow, that first morning the "Eye-Pees" were in conference behind the closed doors of the IP room, discussing all those sorts of things that T-37 IPs discussed behind closed doors.

Looking more closely at the desks in the room, Rick saw that each desk had two student nametags taped on top. Rick found his nametag on the desk of Lieutenant Skip Wipson. Next to his nametag was that of Tony Krawietz, a blond tennis player who had come to Laughlin by way of the Air Force Academy. Tony and Rick took their seats in front of Lieutenant Wipson's desk.

"*Lieutenant* Wipson?" Rick thought. "My instructor is a lieutenant?"

This discovery shocked him. He had always imagined Air Force Instructor Pilots as crusty old officers with thousands of hours of jet time and dozens of combat sorties under their belts. Instead, most IPs at Laughlin were First Assignment Instructor Pilots (FAIPs), new lieutenants on their first tour of duty after a three-month training course at Randolph Air Force Base in San Antonio.

It followed, then, that the instructors were not much older than the students. Some were younger. In spite of this, or, more accurately, because of this, the Air Force demanded that an invisible and impenetrable wall be placed between the instructors and the students. Every interaction was formal. Every conversation ended with "sir" or "ma'am," even if, as often was the case with Bud Jones or Buck Shawhan, the student outranked the instructor.

Rank aside, Rick couldn't help but wonder how it was that he had been assigned to Lieutenant Wipson. His only guess was that it had something to do with the one-page autobiographies Captain Vautrain had asked them to write.

Thinking that somehow the words on those papers would determine their fates as pilots, the students had spent hours on the assignment.

Those in the class who wanted to fly fighters wrote that they would be happy to fly anything just as long as they could fly. This, of course, was a lie. But nobody wanted to come off as cocky.

The Portu-guys, Rick knew, had taken a different approach. They wrote their autobiographies in the poorest hand and lowest grammar they could manage, hoping to establish from the start that their command of English was so limited that they really could not be responsible for any mistakes they made in the program.

With the exception of Thielman, who wrote that he was from Montana and that he was going home as soon as possible to be a fighter pilot, the Guard students crafted their papers particularly delicately. Rick, for instance, after a paragraph explaining his Minnesota origins, had included in his essay such statements as "if things work out" and "provided nothing happens to jeopardize my position" to convey his hopes of flying the fighter he was already assigned.

Glancing at the glass-covered desk and its assortment of flying pictures, water-skiing pictures, tennis pictures, and dollar bills decorated with glued-on magazine clippings, Rick found a clue to what aspect of his autobiography had landed him at this desk. There, at the bottom of the glass, was a set of pictures of what looked like a camping trip along Minnesota's Lake Superior.

Rick's pleasure at being assigned a home-state instructor quickly vanished, however, when next to a picture of Minnesota's Split Rock Lighthouse he saw two pizza delivery job applications with the names *Tony Krawietz* and *Rick Wedan*

already filled in. Rick pointed to them and looked at Tony. Both
grinned nervously.

* * *

The IP room door swung open. Bud Jones, whose rank and
experience had landed him the job of class leader, sang out.
"Room—ten-hut!"

The entire class jumped to attention. Bud reported the Modern Day Cowboys "all present" to Captain Jonathan Straight,
the B-flight commander. Captain Straight told them to take their
seats, welcomed them to the *Killer Bees,* and commenced with
their first morning brief.

Throughout their year at UPT, morning briefs would give
the Modern Day Cowboys the chance to meet once a day as a
class to talk about the local airfield and weather conditions that
might affect that day's flying. After the morning brief, the class
would split apart for academic instruction, individual briefing
with their instructors, and flying. Morning briefs provided con-
tinuity. Morning briefs made them a flight.

One of the main features of the morning brief was safety.
Every morning the flight's safety officer read reports of recent
Air Force mishaps. It was from such reports, they were told,
that all the procedures, regulations, and rules in the Air Force
were derived. In the beginning, there had been no rules. Then
came the first accident, followed shortly thereafter by the first
rule. There were no new kinds of accidents out there, just new
names.

To keep theirs from being added to this list of names, every
day at morning brief the students went through one of the most
important and most intimidating features of pilot training: the
morning stand-up Emergency Procedure (EP). This was the same
procedure introduced at FISHPOT, but at UPT the stand-up was
taken to another level. At UPT, both the emergency situations

and the methods for handling them became quite complicated. At UPT solving the stand-up became something of an art.

The first challenge the new T-37 students faced was the infamous T-37 spin Boldface, a procedure so important to UPT success that many Air Force pilots found themselves able to recite it twenty years after earning their wings.

For the longest time Rick found just writing the spin Boldface to be a challenge. Even more daunting was the prospect of reciting it correctly, in its entirety, while standing at attention in front of the entire class. Even a simple lapse in syntax would mean being "sat down"—and being grounded for the day.

Naturally, this procedure was chosen for the first morning brief. Lieutenant Lea Wrazidlo was in charge of the stand-up. She didn't even bother sugarcoating the challenge by setting up the emergency scenario. She just stood up and said, "Today's stand-up is the spin Boldface. Lieutenant Krawietz, you have the aircraft."

Rick saw just a blur as Tony sprang to attention and blurted "Ma'am, the Boldface for the spin is:

Throttles—Idle

Rudder and Ailerons—Neutral

Stick—Abruptly Full Aft and Hold

Rudder—Abruptly Apply Rudder Opposite Spin Direction
     (Opposite Turn Needle) and Hold

Stick—Abruptly Full Forward One Turn After Applying Rudder

Controls—Neutral After Spinning Stops and Recover From Dive."

Rick winced. Tony had forgotten that he needed the word "full" between "apply" and "rudder."

Lieutenant Wrazidlo hadn't. "Have a seat, Lieutenant Krawietz," she said. "That was very poor. How can we trust you to recover a spinning jet in the air if you can't even tell me how to do it here on the ground? Let's see…Lieutenant Paz—you have the aircraft."

There were eighteen sighs of relief as the Portuguese officer snapped smartly to attention. Paz said nothing, but as Rick watched him, he could see Paz's face work itself into a model of stark confusion. Rick smiled to himself, knowing what his foreign friend had in mind.

"Lieutenant Paz," Lieutenant Wrazidlo repeated, "you have the aircraft."

A glistening bead of sweat rose on Paz's Latin forehead. After an eternity, Paz spoke—in English even worse than he had used at FISHPOT.

"Spin, ahh, Boldface," he began, his mouth straining to darken his speech with Portuguese accent, "I not understand this words. Oh, sorry, sorry. I no cannot explain English."

Lieutenant Wrazidlo didn't lose a beat. In one smooth motion she stepped from behind the podium and pointed at the poor Portuguese student whose government had paid one heck of a lot of money to put him there. "Listen," she said, "I don't know who you are, where you're from, or what it is you think you're doing, but if you can't get the Boldface right, you're not going to fly, ever. Take your seat."

Paz sat down, deflated. His English improved remarkably thereafter.

* * *

Not all EPs would be as succinct and to the point as Lieutenant Wrazidlo's was that first day. As the class progressed through training the students would be confronted with scenarios of ever-increasing complexity.

Sometimes just figuring out what the emergency really was ended up being the hardest part of the stand-up. Other times figuring out how to solve it was the hardest part. Occasionally there was a gap of four or five seconds between coming to an understanding of what the emergency situation was and

coming to an understanding of how to handle it. In such cases
the students' heads filled up with every memorized passage they
had ever learned. They remembered lines from high school
plays, old nursery rhymes, and, appropriately, a multitude of
childhood prayers.

When they were fortunate, one of these memories ended
up being the proper Boldface for the procedure. When they
were unfortunate and couldn't think of anything, it was time to
scramble.

There were many ways to scramble. Tony Krawietz demonstrated one a few weeks into the program when asked what he
would do if, while flying cross country, his jet developed excessive oil pressure. "Well," replied Tony, "I probably wouldn't
notice it, so I wouldn't do anything."

The result: "Have a seat, Lieutenant Krawietz."

Instead of such unvarnished honesty, Tony would have done
well to have taken a lesson from Jeff Cantrell, a lieutenant in
the Modern Day Cowboys and a former Army helicopter pilot
turned good. Jeff had seen the light when he realized that, when-
ever he worked with Air Force A-10 pilots, they would land at
an airport at the end of the day and drive off to hotels for the
night while he and the other helicopter pilots camped out in
the field. The way he figured it, if you landed in the dirt, you
would sleep in the dirt. So he had quit the Army, earned some
money flying off oil rigs in the Gulf of Mexico, and finished up
college with an ROTC commission and an Air Force pilot slot.
Jeff did not want to fly a fighter. He wanted to fly something big
and comfortable with a yoke and a place to put his coffee. Something that didn't land in the dirt.

Jeff brought some of his Army evasion skills with him into
UPT. The first time Jeff demonstrated them was for a difficult
EP presented by Lieutenant Meehan, the flight's safety officer.
Soon after takeoff, the scenario began, the T-37 had hit a large
eagle with a rattlesnake in its talons. The eagle had come through

the canopy and disintegrated. The student's instructor had been rendered unconscious. The rattlesnake had survived and was coiled up on the floor at the instructor's feet.

"Yes, sir," said Jeff as he rose to attention, checklist in hand. "I'd just like to clarify the situation." He then commenced to repeat not only the initial scenario given by Lieutenant Meehan but also the ill-fated steps taken by his three predecessors who had been "sat-down." The recitation lasted almost five minutes. "That's the way I understand the situation," he concluded. "Is that correct?"

"Yes," answered a noticeably impatient Lieutenant Meehan. "Now solve the problem and bring us to a logical conclusion."

"Well, sir," replied Jeff, "I'd maintain aircraft control, analyze the situation, take appropriate action, and land as soon as conditions permitted."

"Okay," prompted Lieutenant Meehan, "go ahead."

"Yes, sir," continued Jeff. "To maintain aircraft control, I'm going to simply fly straight ahead by maintaining my pitch attitude with the stick. I shouldn't need any rudders because both engines are running. What was the weather, again, sir?"

"Clear. The weather is clear."

"Good. Then I would continue to maintain aircraft control by controlling my pitch attitude with the stick. If the weather were bad, then I'd have to worry about flying on instruments or maybe turning before I entered the clouds because I wouldn't want to enter them with a snake in the cockpit."

"The weather is clear," interrupted Lieutenant Meehan. Jeff was pushing the instructor to the limit.

"Yes, then I'd have to look at my engine instruments. What is my oil pressure?"

"Fifty psi," replied Lieutenant Meehan.

Jeff looked up from his checklist with a confused expression. "Both engines?" he asked.

"Yes."

"And my exhaust gas temperature?"

"Normal."

"Both engines?"

"Yes."

"My engine rpm?"

"Normal," snapped Lieutenant Meehan. "Everything is normal, but you have a snake in the cockpit!"

"What color is the snake?"

"I don't know," Lieutenant Meehan answered, then paused, thinking. It seemed that the momentum had shifted. "It's brown," he continued. "It's a brown rattlesnake."

"Does it appear to be a native snake of this region?"

"Yes, yes it does."

"And what do I do with the snake?"

"You climb to twenty thousand feet to make the snake hypoxic and then pull five g's to pin it against the floor so you can grab it and put it in your helmet bag."

"Do I declare an emergency?"

"Yes."

"When I come back to land, do I fly a straight-in or an overhead approach?"

"A straight-in."

"What do I do about my IP?"

"He is unconscious when you land, and you take him to the flight surgeon."

"Do I get my picture in the paper because everyone thinks I'm a hero?"

"Yes."

"May I be seated?"

"Yes, you may."

"Thank you, sir."

Apparently the EP was over, though nobody in the room had any idea what had happened. But they all knew one thing:

Jeff Cantrell would never be given another stand-up as long as Lieutenant Meehan was doing the giving.

* * *

Such EP techniques didn't come to the class out of thin air; they came from experience. On that first day, however, the class had no experience, and nearly everyone had missed some part of spin Boldface by the time Bud Jones finally got the wording right.

Being grounded that first day didn't matter too much because they wouldn't even be eligible to fly until they finished their initial flightline ground training. Still, nobody liked being sat down in front of the class, so it was a group of dejected students that Captain Straight addressed when he again stepped to the podium. He read the daily operations notes from the squadron commander and then, after a few of his own words of motivation, ended the brief and dismissed the students to begin ground training with their IPs.

After dismissal, Captain Straight had only one question: "Where's Thielman, the fighter pilot?" Greg raised his hand. "Would you come into my office, please?" Rick grimaced as he turned to watch the office door close behind his friend. Greg was in for it now.

Ten minutes later Greg emerged from the office. He didn't look like he was in trouble. He was smiling.

It wasn't until after the full twelve-hour day of ground training that Rick was able to ask what words had been exchanged in the office.

"Was he mad at you for bragging that you would be going back home to fly the F-16?" Rick inquired.

"Nah," replied Greg.

"Well, what did he say?"

"He was just telling me a story about how he had been a happy F-16 pilot himself until a couple months ago when Air

Training Command came knocking at his door. He said when that happens, you can either shut the door in their face or let them in, but either way you're going back to pilot training to be an instructor."

"So," Rick pressed, "what did he want?"

"What do you think he wanted? He wanted to know if I could get him into my unit."

"Did you tell him that you could?"

"Of course."

"Can you?"

"Of course not."

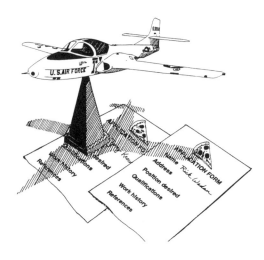

CHAPTER IX

Pogo Pool

If you think your student is ready to solo,
You've waited too long.

— Lieutenant Dan Meehan, Tweet IP

IF THERE WAS ANY AXIOM that Rick proved at UPT, it was that although flying could be learned, it could not be taught, at least not efficiently. Teaching someone to fly could take forever; learning to fly could be accomplished in only a few seconds of revelation.

Almost all of Rick's instruction took place in the hundreds of hours he spent in the classroom or in front of Lieutenant Wipson's desk. Almost all of his learning took place in the relatively few hours he spent in the air.

There was, however, one bridge between classroom instruction and combustion of jet fuel. It was the simulator, and during the course of the year, Rick logged more than 200 hours in the machine designed to give students the valuable lessons of experience while providing them with the even more valuable option of a reset button.

* * *

Laughlin's simulators were housed a block away from the squadron building. There were six T-37 and six T-38 full-motion, full-visual simulators, each supported by massive hydraulic pistons.

Civilian-contract simulator operators oversaw the operation from a large deck high above the machines. Once student and instructor were safely aboard, the operator commanded the access ramp to lift away, leaving the simulator free to move.

To make the simulator experience true to life, the students were required to wear helmets, gloves, seatbelts, and parachutes. The instructors wore only headphones for communication. Out of prudence they also wore seatbelts, because the simulator, being true to life, simulated not only flying, but crashing as well.

The controls in the simulator were also true to life. The only real difference between the cockpit of the simulator and the cockpit of the jet was the addition of a certain small panel in the simulator. By manipulating the panel's two round dials, the instructors could call up all sorts of malfunctions to test the students' abilities to put into practice what they had learned to articulate in the stand-up. It didn't take long for Rick and his friends to take to calling this instructor control panel *dial-a-death*.

* * *

Rick was the first of the Modern Day Cowboys to graduate from the T-37 simulator to the T-37 itself. Although he credited his pole position to the stick powers he had displayed in the simulator, in reality he achieved this honor due to the simple fact that his IP, Lieutenant Wipson, held arguably the most powerful position in the flight: He was the scheduler.

At UPT the flight scheduler controlled the students' lives. With the help of the magnetic scheduling board, the scheduler determined when they would fly, where they would fly, and, most importantly, with whom they would fly.

The first time Rick saw his name on the scheduling board was for his dollar ride. This first flight was not graded. On the rest of the flights, the instructor would fill out a computer-calculated bubble scoresheet during debrief, giving each task accomplished one of four possible grades: "E" for excellent, "G" for good, "F" for fair, or "U" for unsatisfactory.

On the dollar ride Rick could take the jet with no pressure, fly around for awhile to get the feel of it, and then come back, overwhelmed, with a clear realization of how much harder he was going to have to work if he was to make it through the program.

Because the ride was not graded, tradition dictated that the instructor charge the student for the privilege of flying the jet. The charge was a dollar. That explained the collection of dressed-up and decorated dollar bills that Rick had seen under the glass of Lieutenant Wipson's desk.

* * *

When the sun finally came up on the morning of Rick's dollar ride, it didn't actually come out but merely illuminated a solidly overcast sky with a ceiling of less than 500 feet. This was unfortunate, but it didn't preclude the flight. They could fly on instruments.

The weather was only one of his many concerns as Rick went through the steps leading up to his dollar ride. The first order of business after being dismissed from the morning brief was to sit down and listen to Lieutenant Wipson discuss how they would take off, what they would do in the practice area, and what kind of landings they would make. The brief also included a quick review of how they would handle any emergencies during the flight. If they had an emergency, the instruction would end, and Lieutenant Wipson and he would act as a team to get the jet safely back on the ground.

After the brief, Rick walked with Lieutenant Wipson to the scheduling desk and grabbed the small magnetic "puck" with his name on it from the scheduling board. Making sure he also had his checklist and inflight guide, Rick followed Lieutenant Wipson down the hall to the sign-out desk.

When Rick gave the duty officer his puck and told her he was flying with Lieutenant Wipson for his dollar ride, she pulled Lieutenant Wipson's own puck off the wall and placed it alongside Rick's on a big magnetic board next to a jet number and parking location. Then, as she handed Rick a bag containing the required in-flight publications, she turned to Lieutenant Wipson and asked, "Do you want me to call the firetrucks now and tell them it's Lieutenant Wedan's first ride?"

"Nah," Lieutenant Wipson replied as he skimmed through the publications to make sure they were current. "I think it's better training for the emergency crews if we surprise them every once in awhile. I am going to send him out for a bucket of *prop wash* and a roll of *flight line*, though." Lieutenant Wipson could be pretty funny when he wanted to be.

With their publications in hand, Lieutenants Wipson and Wedan stepped from the scheduling area into the parachute room. There, among the hundred or so neatly spaced cabinets, they found their parachutes and helmets. They hoisted their chutes to their backs and grabbed their helmets, helmet bags, and headset hearing protectors. Before stepping out the door, they tested their masks for valving and radio connections—Lieutenant Wipson with the quick certainty of a well-learned habit pattern, Rick with the unsure fumbling of a first-time student.

The door behind the test station opened to a sidewalk leading to a green park bench on the flightline. There, after a few minutes of waiting, Lieutenant Wipson and Rick hopped into the blue Air Force van that took them to their assigned T-37.

After the bus dropped them off and they located their jet, Lieutenant Wipson opened a panel on the side of the Tweet, flipped a switch, and watched the canopy open. Mimicking his instructor's every move, Rick removed his heavy parachute and placed it, straps up, on the wing of the jet. Rick then checked the cockpit to ensure that all ejection seat safety pins were installed before beginning the walkaround inspection.

This wasn't the first time Rick had performed a walkaround of the T-37. Captain Vautrain had taught the class how to do the inspection during systems academics. Since then, Rick had done it all a million times in the comfort of his recliner. Known as "chair-flying," this mental practice consisted of sitting in a chair at home and mentally going through every step of an upcoming flight. The preflight wasn't really flying, but it was where flying started, so Rick had practiced it every day—in his head.

Neither Lieutenant Wipson nor Rick found anything wrong with the jet. So, after checking over the aircraft maintenance logbook, they strapped on their parachutes and climbed into the Tweet.

Two feelings flooded Rick as the crew chief helped him attach his harness and plug in his mask. The first was claustrophobia. There were straps and hoses everywhere. Rick had never felt so confined in all his life. He could barely move.

The second was confusion. This wasn't the Champ. There were switches and dials and gauges laid out all over the instrument panel in front of him. They came as a shocking surprise. He might have seen them somewhere before—in textbooks, or in the simulator—but here in the jet, with all the noise of the flightline, with all his gear on his back, with all the excitement of the moment, any sense of familiarity evaporated.

The checklist strapped to his leg saved him. One glance at it confirmed that he at least remembered how to read, and that gave him the confidence to continue.

Following the black and yellow pages, Rick moved surely, but slowly, through the starting checklist. He checked the warning lights, the fuel, and the switch positions. He checked that the control lock that held the stick rigid on the ground was properly swung and stowed out of the way.

With these checks complete, Rick was ready to start the jet. After receiving clearance from the crew chief outside, Rick flipped and held a spring-loaded switch with his left forefinger.

The battery turned the starter-generator on the left engine. Rick lifted another spring-loaded switch to begin the ignition process. At the first rumble, he removed his finger from the ignition switch. At 22 percent rpm, he took his finger off the starter-generator switch as the turbine spun to life.

Rick repeated the process with the right engine.

Both Lieutenant Wipson and Rick removed their ejection seat safety pins and showed them to the crew chief. Rick pulled and displayed the single canopy jettison pin from above the left throttles. The crew chief gave him a thumbs-up; they were ready to taxi.

Working his way down to the runway with his forefinger depressing the nosewheel steering button on his control stick, Rick had to run through another whole set of checks. He had to check once again that he was strapped in, that he had fuel, and that all of his instruments were working properly.

Many of these checks fell into the category known as "challenge and response." That meant that Rick not only had to perform the check, but also had to confirm that Lieutenant Wipson had done the same.

"Sir, my seat belt, shoulder harness, and zero delay are connected," Rick said over the intercom.

"My seat belt, shoulder harness, and zero delay are connected," Lieutenant Wipson replied.

"Sir, my regulator is working, I'm showing on, normal, normal, good blinker, pressure is fifty psi."

"My regulator is also working. On, normal, normal, good blinker, fifty psi."

What with all these checks, Rick was exhausted by the time they had traversed the taxiway. He had already done more checking and confirming than in all of his Champ flights put together—and he hadn't even left the ground.

With his energy thus drained, Rick felt as if he could entertain only two or at the most three thoughts at the same time.

One was how much his nose hurt because of the mask. The other was how he couldn't move because of all the harnesses and straps that engulfed him. This left Rick with only one synapse left to devote to flying the jet. Where were the days of flying in jeans, lumberjack shirts, and baseball caps?

* * *

Rick recovered once he was cleared for takeoff. In fact, the sound of pushing up the power of the two J-69 engines was so exciting that Rick forgot, at least for the moment, how terribly uncomfortable he was. He also forgot to raise his landing gear after takeoff and to switch radio frequencies before talking to departure control. Good thing the ride wasn't graded.

Once they entered the weather on climb-out, Lieutenant Wipson took control of the jet. This was good because, as soon as they went in the clouds, Rick was instantly and totally disoriented. "Just look at the attitude indicator," directed Lieutenant Wipson. "Make that be your world." Rick tried, but he couldn't quite make himself believe that the little gyroscopic ball was the world. It indicated that they were flying straight and level. The fluids in his inner ear, on the other hand, were telling him they were in a sixty-degree right-hand bank.

By the time they arrived in the practice area this feeling had largely subsided, due mostly to the fact that they had emerged from the clouds and were now in the clear, sandwiched between two solid decks of clouds.

"Go ahead and do anything you want," Lieutenant Wipson told Rick as he gave his student control of the jet. This was the kind of offer Rick had dreamed of. "Here's an Air Force jet; go ahead and do whatever you want in it." Wow!

After only a split second of thought, Rick decided to do a barrel roll. He had often done these in the Champ, both because they were fun and because they were the only acrobatic maneuver he could do in the Champ and be reasonably certain that no pieces would fall off.

Just as John had taught him, with both hands Rick jammed the stick to the left as fast and as far as he could.

"Wow," Rick thought as he neutralized the stick to stop the roll, "this thing rolls pretty fast." In fact, the jet had rolled so rapidly that Rick was a little disoriented. He thought it best to pull back on the stick and climb some while he sorted things out.

What Rick failed to realize was that he hadn't done a single roll. He had done one-and-a-half rolls. This left him inverted and pulling not up but down into the cloud layer below him. If he could have seen through the clouds, he would have noticed that the houses were getting bigger.

The maneuver wasn't a total failure, however. It taught him that, when properly applied by a qualified instructor, the out-of-control recoveries they were learning did, in fact, work. It also taught him that the maximum airspeed limitations in the Dash-1 weren't really maximums at all. They could quite easily be exceeded.

* * *

More than anything, Rick's dollar ride gave him a reference point from which to chair-fly. Between his dollar ride and his first real sortie, Rick just about wore out his recliner. Sitting there for hours on end, Rick rocked back and forth, muttering inflight checks to himself, moving his hands on imaginary controls, making imaginary radio calls. Hundreds of times Rick flew his T-37 up initial, pitched out, lowered the gear and speedbrake, and flew flawless overhead patterns. He flew normal patterns, single engine patterns, and no-flap patterns—each time moving the throttles and stick smoothly and delicately to precisely hold glidepath and airspeed. His flying time was limited, but he could always get another chair.

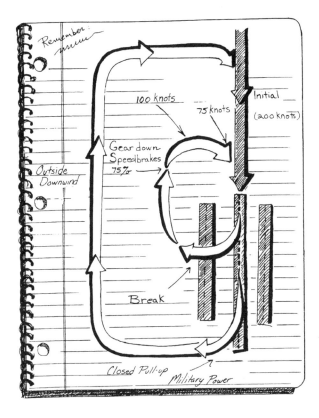

On his eleventh ride in the program, just a few days before Christmas, Rick's hard work paid off. That was the day he soloed an Air Force jet—and learned the first big lesson of UPT.

This first solo was called a "Pogo Ride" because that was the call sign that the pilot had to use. When flying rides with an instructor, the students at Laughlin used the call sign "Tiger." Advanced solo students used the call sign "Cash." Both of these were relatively proud-sounding call signs. But not Pogo. Pogo made the insecure pilot feel stupid and self-conscious at the same time, which, of course, was the intent. Not even the most reckless student in the world could be a hot dog in the pattern with a call sign like Pogo.

* * *

Rick was a little nervous on the day of his Pogo ride, but he was also pretty sure that his survival instincts would fill in any voids left in his training. This turned out to be the case.

After a few warm-up touch-and-goes, Rick landed the jet, pulled off the runway, shut down the right engine, and kicked his instructor out. In accordance with tradition, just before he walked away, Lieutenant Wipson ripped his wings from the Velcro on his chest and handed them to his student. This was only fitting, of course, because if Rick crashed, Lieutenant Wipson would probably lose his wings anyway.

After an uneventful solo takeoff, Rick received clearance for a closed pattern. Pulling back quickly on the stick, Rick started the jet's nose pitching up, noticing as he did that without Lieutenant Wipson sitting next to him, the cockpit was not quiet, as he had expected, but strangely loud. Replacing Lieutenant Wipson's admonitions were clanks, hums, and vibrations he had never heard before.

Despite this, Rick was more relaxed than he had been in the past two weeks. For the first time, there wasn't someone watching everything he did, judging him, grading him—at least not from within the jet.

Of course, as a Pogo, Rick was never really unmonitored. This was because the Pogo ride was a pattern-only sortie. In the closed pattern Rick was only a mile away from the tower. In the outside box, a rectangular pattern precisely defined by ground references, Rick was farther away but still in plain view of the base.

Part of this monitoring was the pattern procedure that required Rick to verify that he had lowered his landing gear prior to turning the base leg to final approach. Because the pattern was usually extremely busy, once he made this call he would be automatically cleared to land unless sent around for some reason. One such reason might be a jet on the runway in front of him. Another might be that he had forgotten to lower his landing gear.

The controllers in the Runway Supervisory Unit (RSU) would know that he had forgotten his gear because there were students in the RSU box doing nothing but watching every plane with binoculars to make sure nobody landed gear-up. Usually pulling such tours was an exercise in monotony. Because usually, everybody lowered their gear. But not always.

* * *

Just as Lieutenant Wipson had taught him, Rick banked his Tweet to the right and pulled it over to parallel the inside runway, leveling off at the pattern altitude of 2,100 feet. At the midfield point Rick extended the speedbrakes. Just as he was about to reach for the gear handle, as he had chair-flown a thousand times, Rick heard "Tiger 34 flight of two, initial" over the radio.

This call meant that a flight of two T-37s—Tiger 34 by name—was flying straight up the runway at pattern altitude. They wouldn't be in conflict with him. Just the same, Rick scanned the horizon for the jets.

By the time he spied the two aircraft in the distance, Rick was already at the perch point where he needed to begin his descending turn to final approach and make his "gear down" call to the RSU. Rick keyed the microphone. "Pogo 25, gear down."

Even as these words escaped his mouth, Rick's soul filled with terror at the sight of his gear handle. It should have been down with three green lights. It wasn't. It was up with a single red light. That's when Rick remembered the meaning of the

warning horn that was beeping in his helmet. In his fixation
with finding the other jets, Rick hadn't lowered his landing gear.

The gear handle swelled to approximately twenty times its
normal size. Before, it had been the size of a golf ball. Now it
looked like a basketball. Reaching up with both hands Rick
wrestled the enormous handle into the correct position. With
bated breath he watched the gear indicator lights turn to one,
two, and finally three green lights as he rolled out on final. Rick
waited for the "go-around" from the RSU controller, the fateful
ground-to-air missile that would tell him and the rest of the listening world that he had failed the ride.

It never came. He had caught his mistake in time. The RSU
observers hadn't noticed. Rick had almost tried to land without
landing gear, but nobody was the wiser. Nobody, that is, except for Lieutenant Rick Wedan, who in a few short seconds in
the air had learned more than weeks of ground instruction had
been able to teach.

* * *

As Rick got off the crew bus following his flight, he was met by
the whole of class 92-01. Together they grabbed him, stripped
off his parachute and helmet, and dragged him to the large cor-
rugated-steel watering tank used to baptize the new solo students. With one powerful throw, Rick was in the cool water of
the Pogo Pool. His wallet was soaked and he might need a new
watch. But he didn't mind. He was, at last, a jet pilot.

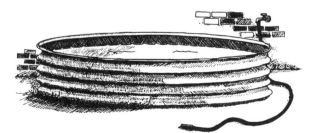

CHAPTER X

Check, Please

*Half the trouble in this world comes from trying to
figure out how to change things that can't be
changed on account of having happened.*

–Kenneth Roberts, *Rabble in Arms*

BEFORE RICK WENT OFF TO LAUGHLIN, Dave Allen had warned him
that pilot training would be an emotional roller coaster. In the
morning, he'd be on top of the world. In the afternoon, he'd
feel like the biggest fool that same world had ever seen.

Rick found this to be true, with one addition. He found that
going through pilot training was like riding a roller coaster, at
night, with no lights. During a daytime roller coaster ride, he
thought, if you opened your eyes, you could see what was coming. You would know when you were on top. You would know
when you were about to go down. You would know when it
was time to raise your hands above your head. You would know
when it was time to scream.

At night, you couldn't see what the roller coaster had in
store. All you could do was flop down your ticket, strap in, and
hope that the engineers hadn't put any bars low enough to hit
you on the head. And you had better not relax—because as
soon as you thought you were on top to stay, *whoosh*, out
dropped the bottom.

* * *

At UPT, the prime mover of this cycle of emotions was something called a checkride.

Checkrides at UPT determined the future. If a student rose to the occasion on those few rides, his future looked bright. If, however, he flew out of the wrong side of the bed at the sound of his early-morning alarm on the day of the checkride, he could be in serious trouble. Because if he hooked a checkride, the gears of elimination would begin to turn.

The first revolution would be a trip to the flight commander's office. The next would be a practice ride designed to fix whatever problem had caused the initial failure. For some unfathomable reason of accounting, this ride had the name 87.

After the 87, the student would be given an 88 Initial Progress Check with the assistant squadron commander. If the student passed this ride, he would be returned to the land of the living to continue with his class. If he didn't, he would get two more 87s and the chance to fly an 89 Final Progress Check with the squadron commander.

There was no 90.

As Rick learned through the grapevine, some mistakes were automatic hooks on a checkride. These included scaring the check pilot in any way and the all-too-common "going out of the practice area." A student could do picture-perfect spin recovery, but if on a checkride he accidentally reached for the magazine rack instead of the toilet paper and went out of the area, he'd probably be meeting his assistant squadron commander.

* * *

Rick's first two checkrides, his Midphase and Final Contact checks, reminded him of the Champ days. They tested his contact flying—his ability to take off, fly to the area, perform acrobatics, stalls, and spin recoveries, and come back and land. By the time he took these checks, he was an expert at these things. On these checks, his innate stick power served him well.

Then came the instrument check.

The week before his instrument checkride, Rick was engulfed in the standard pre-checkride anxiety. The thought of the ride consumed him. He spent every spare minute—and these were precious and few when living a twelve-hour duty day— boning up on the thousands of questions he thought the check pilot might ask. He nearly wore out the mechanism of his chair as he rocked through every possible instrument profile he might face.

When the day of the checkride finally came, it was a relief just to have an end to the constant studying. When the day of the checkride finally came, Rick was ready.

To lull him into complacency, the checkride started out fine. As was usual, Rick's stomach was filled with butterflies during his preflight check. But as he signaled the crew chief to remove the chocks, his anxiety disappeared. His confidence returned. Now all he had to do was fly.

Takeoff was normal. As soon as Rick got the gear up, he gave control of the jet to the check pilot and put on his instrument visor, the canvas flap he had to wear over his helmet to keep him from looking outside and force him to navigate solely off of instruments. With the hood securely in place, Rick took the jet back and flew the standard instrument departure out to one of the practice areas just as he had done dozens of times before.

In the practice area things went fine. Rick demonstrated his mastery of instruments by flying the precise climbing and descending turns known as the Vertical-S. Rick performed steep turns skillfully and recovered the jet quickly from the unusual attitudes the check pilot set up for him.

Rick then proceeded to a nearby Rocksprings county airport to shoot a short and simple instrument procedure. After completing an error-free approach, Rick called on the radio for climbout instructions back to Laughlin, expecting a gold medal for the mental gymnastics he was displaying. He thought he had it made. That was his first mistake.

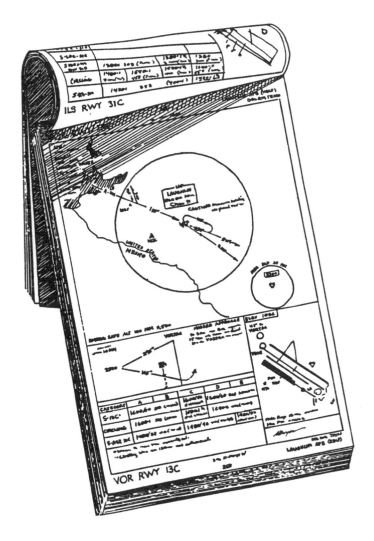

His second was being inflexible when instructed to intercept the Laughlin 057 radial inbound. Every other time Rick had shot the approach he had been cleared immediately to a certain holding fix at Laughlin. Proceeding via a radial threw him off. It didn't fit in with his plan. He hadn't chair-flown it.

While fixating on the procedure for intercepting a radial inbound, Rick committed the classic mistake of an instrument pilot. He forgot to change his navigation radio receiver to the correct station. He hadn't switched it to Laughlin, but had left it set for Rocksprings.

Rick stared at his instruments. Nothing made sense. He wasn't even sure he was still in Texas. He started to sweat. His temperature rose. It looked like the beginning of the most dangerous emergency a student pilot could have—a helmet fire. Panicking, Rick banked the airplane back and forth trying to make the instruments read right. Finally it dawned on him what was wrong. With shaking hands Rick tuned in the correct station and proceeded toward the holding fix. Unfortunately, dwelling on the mistake he had just made, he dialed in the wrong radial for the fix. He should have put in 270. Instead, he dialed the reciprocal, 090.

Without warning, the check pilot spoke. "You sure you have the right radial dialed in?" he asked. The words mortified Rick. Other than the required challenge and response items, this was the first thing he had ever heard a check pilot say in a jet. Rick looked down at the Course Indicator needle and groaned.

As Rick considered the ramifications of his misdial, he turned the wrong direction into the holding pattern. This mistake Rick figured out himself, but by then it was too late. The ride was over, he was sure. The rest was just paperwork.

By the time they were back on the ground, Rick had given up. All he hoped for was that he would soon awaken and find that it had all been a bad dream and that he could start the whole day over.

When the check pilot gave him his ground evaluation EP of an overheat warning light during takeoff, Rick, wallowing in self-pity, completely missed the fact that it was associated with smoke in the cockpit. The Dash-1 required that such a situation be considered a fire and that the engine be shut down. Rick knew that. He had gone through the exact Emergency Procedure dozens of times with Lieutenant Wipson in preparation for the checkride. Rick had always done it right. But not this time.

A few minutes later, the ground evaluation ended and the check pilot pulled out a gradesheet and began filling in bubbles. Rick was mesmerized by the movement of the check pilot's hands. When the movement stopped, the check pilot handed Rick the gradesheet. "I thought you flew a really nice jet," he said. "You made a few mistakes, but they were nothing big." The examiner paused. Rick's heart stopped while he waited for the next words.

"I'm going to have to hook you on the ride, though, because you didn't shut down that engine in the EP. It's clear and simple in the Dash-1. If there is smoke associated with the overheat light, you have to shut down the engine. My hands are tied. Here's your gradesheet. Do you have any questions about the eighty-eight or what is going to happen to you in the future?"

"No," Rick said, dropping his head in dismay. The future was the last thing he wanted to think about.

* * *

Twenty-four hours before the ill-fated checkride, Rick had flown a solo proficiency ride, practicing the Thunderbird tryout maneuvers he had been working on for months. Lieutenant Wipson had tried to tell him that he should use the time to practice his acrobatic maneuvers to "visually orient himself to many changing flight attitudes" as the training regulation said. But Rick hadn't thought of that regulation when he got out to the area; he had thought about the regulation Captain Eddie Rickenbacker had followed in World War I: Basic Battle Aerobatics and Trick Flying.

Soaring around and around the clouds, Rick had thought to himself, I am the greatest! I am the king of the sky! I am the master of this machine and all I survey! He performed Loops, Immelmanns and Cloverleafs. He flew fast. He flew upside down. For twenty minutes, Second Lieutenant Rick Wedan was the greatest jet pilot of all time. He couldn't imagine that any other way of life had ever held any appeal. Racing through the sky, he forgot that any other life existed at all. He forgot his earthbound cares. He forgot his earthbound ambitions. Rick shouted for joy as he climbed and rolled and looped. Roller coasters didn't get any higher than this.

Now, one hour after leaving the check pilot's office, Rick sat on the edge of his bed bouncing his basketball off his dorm room's concrete wall, wishing he hadn't bought his new stereo because he'd need the money when he washed out of pilot training for not being able to fly instruments. Sitting there alone, Rick gathered his depression around him like a blanket. His roller coaster had hit rock bottom.

There was only one direction to turn—toward his old friend Matthew J. Schuster.

Matt had been selected to fly F-16s for the Green Mountain Boys in Vermont. He was a few months behind Rick in training, however, and had arrived just the week before at FISHPOT in San Antonio. Rick had planned on driving over to San Antonio on Saturday so Matt could help him celebrate success on his final T-37 checkride. Now it wouldn't be much of a celebration.

But what the heck, Rick thought. He might as well go. It wasn't as if he needed to study any more. He had practically worn out his books as well as his easy chair preparing for the checkride. And anyway, no amount of study could protect him from his own stupidity. Besides, Rick couldn't take being around jets for another second. So, throwing a small overnight bag into the passenger seat of his wagon, Rick took off through the desert to San Antonio.

Driving along the lightly traveled highway Rick tried to rationalize that somehow hooking the ride had been positive. But the more he thought about it, the more he realized that failure could never be good. Failure might build character, he admitted, but character meant little to a fighter pilot. And that's what Rick wanted to be. So he resolved that this failure would have only one effect on his life—to ensure that it never happened again.

The first step, he figured, was to try to put the events of the day behind him. Maybe some music. Rick searched through his cluttered glovebox for likely cassettes. There, among Hank Williams, Jr. and Boston, Rick found what appeared to be just the ticket—a stress management cassette called *Let It Go*. He had no idea how it had gotten in his car, but there it was.

With a *kerchunk*, the player swallowed the tape.

After several seconds of hissing, Rick heard soft chimes and what sounded like a light breeze through tall trees. Then came the softest, mellowest, most soothing voice he had ever heard.

"Relaaaax. Relaaaax. Breathe deep. Hold it. Hold it. Let go. Relaaaax. Relax your shoulders. Let your cares drain away. Relax your neck. Do you feel the stress leaving you?"

Hmm, Rick thought. Not bad so far.

"Think back on your day. Were you good to yourself? Think back on your morning. Did you treat yourself well?"

Rick thought back on his morning. His shoulders tightened. He thought back on his day. A muscle knotted in his neck. Out came *Let It Go*. In went Hank Williams, Jr.—*Man of Steel.*

* * *

After arriving at the FISHPOT quarters, Rick found his old friend Matt at his dormitory sink draining water from a can of tuna. Holding the can upside down, Matt pressed the detached lid against the chunks inside and without looking up asked, "How did the checkride go?"

Matt was no fool. He knew that Rick's world, like the world of any student at pilot training, revolved around flying. That's all students at pilot training thought about. That's all students at pilot training talked about. To ask about anything else would be the most trivial of small talk, particularly after a checkride.

"I hooked," Rick confessed.

At that Matt squeezed his thumb too hard on the tuna lid, bent it, and sent the whole mess flying into the sink. He turned to Rick. "What happened?"

"I don't know," Rick replied, "I just don't know."

* * *

Later that evening, surrounded by Matt and a few of the students from Matt's FISHPOT class, Rick related the events of the ride. He hoped that telling the story would help exorcise some of the evil locked inside him. It did more than that.

To his surprise, the struggling T-41 pilots weren't interested in his failure. He told them he had hooked his ride, but all they heard was that he had hooked it in a jet.

"Wow," one of Matt's friends asked, "what's it like to push up the power on jet engines for takeoff?" Rick wanted to tell him the truth, that except for the sound it really wasn't that much different from pushing up the power of a T-41. On seeing the expectant look on the FISHPOT student's face, however, Rick changed course in mid-sentence. "Oh," he said, "it's really not that much different than, ahh, any fighter. It's pretty impressive. You really get pressed back in your seat." The FISHPOT students stared at Rick in awe, restoring his flagging confidence with their ill-conceived hero worship. He was, after all, a jet pilot.

Matt pushed Rick into the final stage of recovery on Sunday afternoon as Rick prepared to return to Laughlin. "You know," Matt said, "from all the reading I've done about fighter pilots, the best ones are those lucky enough to survive long enough to learn from their mistakes. Remember Erich Hartmann in World War II?"

Rick recalled the countless stories he had heard about the legendary German, the greatest fighter pilot of all time.

"He forgot to check his fuel on his first mission over enemy lines," Matt reminded him. "He ran out of gas and had to crash land his airplane and walk back to his base. He went on to shoot down three-hundred-fifty-two enemy planes."

"Yeah, so?" Rick asked.

"He had to crash to learn his lesson."

"Yeah, I guess you're right," Rick sighed. His friend was right. Maybe an 88 wasn't such a high price to pay after all. Committed to succeed where before he had failed, Rick climbed into his car, gave Matt a wave, and drove off to Del Rio, a Modern Day Cowboy ready to get back in the saddle.

* * *

On Monday morning, Rick met with his Flight Commander. Behind closed doors, Captain Straight counseled him, telling him what could happen if he somehow failed the 88. Also by regulation, he made sure Rick wasn't having any personal problems that might have affected his performance.

"All I did was mess up the EP!" Rick answered defensively, frustrated at this line of questioning.

"I know," replied Captain Straight soothingly, "but I have to ask these questions. Don't worry about anything. I've already spoken to your 88 check pilot and told him that you're one of the best instrument pilots in class and that we have full confidence in you. So just go out there and do a good job."

"Yes, sir," Rick replied, ready to get the heck out of the office.

"Ahh, one more thing, Lieutenant Wedan."

"Yes, sir?"

"Lieutenant Thielman told me that your unit might have some F-16 jobs available. I'm interested in just that sort of thing. Do you think you might be able to help me out?"

"Sir, I'll do everything I can," Rick answered, more determined than ever that it wouldn't be *his* job that Captain Straight took.

Even though it was only Monday, Rick was already tired of telling people that he wasn't having any personal problems—at least none apart from hooking the checkride. He was also tired of having his classmates look at him strangely—worried, no doubt, that his incompetence had come as a result of some strange form of communicable flying disease; a disease that nobody, no physician or healer, could cure. Only Rick could cure it. In the air. With the assistant squadron commander.

* * *

Following an uneventful practice 87, Rick got his chance to clear his name. Sitting next to him in the jet, the assistant squadron commander closely eyed every switch Rick touched and every instrument Rick monitored. Just as on the first flight, Rick made his share of errors. But this time he remembered that he was expected to make some.

This time he didn't get flustered. He corrected his mistakes and focused on the next phase of flight. Most of all he made certain this time that the Laughlin radio frequency was set in before he tried to intercept any radials. And on the ground, he remembered that where there was smoke, there was probably fire. Explaining that he would shut off the engine in accordance with the Dash-1, Rick completed his 88.

When the assistant squadron commander congratulated him on his performance, Rick knew he was one of the lucky ones— he had survived long enough to learn from his mistakes.

His checkride complete, his disease removed, Rick exited the debrief to once again walk boldly in the land of the living—on top of the roller coaster and planning to stay there.

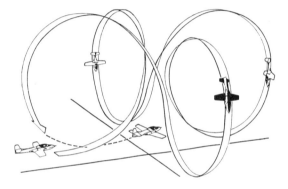

CHAPTER XI

White Rocket

The faster you go,
The faster you go faster.

— Unpublished Logbook of Pilot Training Wisdom

Two weeks after his brief walk through the valley of the shadow of washing out of pilot training, Rick was Tweet Complete. The good thing about this was moving up one more rung on the Air Force ladder. At AMS there had been a lot of talk about what it would be like to fly the T-41. At FISHPOT, the students had wondered if they would ever be able to fly something as amazing as the T-37. Then, when they had finally gotten to the Tweet, the new jet pilots had found themselves gazing admiringly at the T-38 students taxiing by them on the way to the long center runway. In recognition of this admiration, the T-38 students would look down at them in their little Tweets, smile rakishly behind their disconnected oxygen masks, and ever so casually give them a wave.

The T-38 call signs only added to the mystique. In the T-37, "Tiger" had been the best call sign. Rick had felt pretty good about saying "Tiger two one, gear down, full stop." But the T-38 students had that beat by a mile. Their call sign was "Cool."

Relative skill had no place in this hierarchy. Even the worst student ever to pilot the T-38 had one up on the best student in a T-37. The T-38 pilot might be just one day from washing out of pilot training altogether. It didn't matter. The T-38 pilot was Cool, and until the Modern Day Cowboys flew the T-38, they weren't. Not yet.

The bad thing about being Tweet Complete was starting out on the bottom again. Halfway through Tweets, all of Rick's early-on studying had paid off. He knew the Dash-1 by heart. Every number associated with the jet was second nature. The discharge of information that had at first threatened to blow him apart in his attempt to drink from the firehose had diminished to nothing more than a gentle trickle.

Once the Modern Day Cowboys stepped across to the other side of the squadron building and into the White Rocket hallway, however, the firehose was hooked up again—this time to a bigger hydrant.

In the end, the T-37 had been relatively simple. The T-38 was an order of magnitude more complicated. It had hydraulic controls, afterburners, and a whole panel of annunicator lights which, if properly interpreted, could divulge which of the jet's many systems had failed.

The worst part of this for Rick was acknowledging that all the numbers he had spent so long making the most important part of his life were now worthless. And he realized that the numbers he was learning now would also have to be dumped when he moved on to the F-16. Of course, if he didn't master the T-38, he'd never have to worry about learning the F-16.

* * *

Back in the Tweet, Rick had found that he could have numbers and words thrown at him all day, but until he sat in the cockpit and saw what the instructor was talking about, it wouldn't sink in. So as soon as he was allowed to go over to the simulator building to sit in the cockpit trainers, Rick lassoed Greg and did just that.

Probably the most striking feature of the T-38 was its tandem cockpit configuration. In the T-37, they had sat right next to their instructor. Looking at the cockpit trainer, it was clear that in the T-38, they would be sitting all alone at the end of a big old telephone pole. There would still be instructors along for the ride. However, the instructors would be relegated to the backseat—a good ten feet behind their pupils. And student and instructor would be separated not only by distance but by a thick sheet of plastic.

Ostensibly, this plastic existed to protect the instructor in the event of a bird strike to the front cockpit. The Portu-guys knew better. The plastic was there, Paz said, to keep the instructor from reaching up and hitting the student.

Paz drew this conclusion from an experience his father had in a tandem-seat Portuguese trainer. One particularly ill-tempered instructor would unscrew his stick from the back seat and use it to discipline his student.

After several rides with this instructor, Paz's father had enough. So, just before the flight, he went over to a spare aircraft, removed one of its sticks and hid it in his flightsuit. Soon after they took off, the instructor pulled the same old trick. After a couple of blows the young Portuguese student put the airplane in a steep dive, took the spare stick from its hiding place and waved it in his hand. "Sir," he yelled as he threw the stick out the partially open canopy, "if you don't need your stick, then I don't need mine either!"

At that the flustered instructor cussed up a blue streak—which was no doubt quite impressive in Portuguese—and desperately tried to put his own stick back in place as the ground rushed to meet them. The panicked instructor screamed, unable to fix his rear control. At the last minute Paz's father pulled the airplane away from the earth and back to level flight without saying a word. The instructor never hit him again.

* * *

Neither Rick nor Greg fully believed this story, but they did understand the significance of a tandem cockpit arrangement where the instructor did not have access to all the aircraft's systems. Now they had more control. And more responsibility.

To make sure they would be ready for this responsibility, Greg and Rick spent hour after hour in the cockpit trainers going over interior checks, challenge and response items, and emergency procedures.

The two friends spent a lot of their time in the cockpit trainers practicing fuel computations. In the T-38, they would be carrying and burning so much gas that there wasn't an approach speed; there was an approach calculation. For a normal approach, they would fly the final turn at 175 knots plus one knot for every 100 pounds of fuel above 1,000 pounds. Once on final approach, they could slow twenty knots. These equations meant two things to Rick and Greg. They would have to actually think and fly at the same time, and they were going to be flying real fast.

* * *

Rick found out just how fast on his T-38 dollar ride. On that day, as he walked from the T-38 signout desk to the parachute room, he had one simple goal. He wanted to be able to put on his g-suit faster than Lieutenant Thorpe, his newly assigned T-38 IP.

This g-suit was something new. Back in T-37 physiology class, Rick had learned that during tight turns, centrifugal force would make him feel heavy. It was like twirling a ball on a string around his head. The faster he twirled, the harder it would be to hold on to the string. The faster he flew and the tighter the turn he tried to make, the more his body would be pressed into the seat. It was really a question of inertia. Flying straight and level, both he and the airplane were in equilibrium. If he banked and turned sharply, the plane would turn, but his body would want to keep going straight. The force the airplane exerted on him through the seat was called "g" force.

One g was equal to the force that gravity exerted on him every day just being on earth. In a two-g turn, his body would be thrown against the seat as if he weighed two times his normal weight. Four g's, four times his normal weight. In a six-g turn, he would weigh over 1,000 pounds—six times more than his normal weight of 170 pounds. His arms would weigh more, his legs would weigh more, and, significantly, his blood would weigh more. In fact, he was told to expect that in very high-g turns his heart would not be able to generate enough pressure to pump his oxygen-carrying blood up to his head where it was needed.

In the T-37, they hadn't pulled many of these g's. In the T-38, however, they would be pulling five and six g's. That's why they were issued g-suits. During turns, the air bladders within the g-suit's skin-tight, chap-like leggings would inflate with air from the jet's compressor. This would help Rick in his effort to keep the blood from pooling in his legs and stomach.

Overall, the g-suits appeared bulky and grotesque, but to Rick they were beautiful. They were a part of flying the T-38. In addition, Rick knew that throwing the g-suit on in a hurry was part of what it took to be an Alert pilot, so he had been practicing donning the "speed jeans" daily since the life support shop had fitted them to his legs. He had even oiled the zippers. He could have them on in less than a minute.

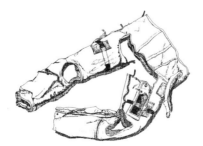

Lieutenant Thorpe found Rick at his locker, chute on, helmet in hand, struggling with his partially zipped g-suit. Rick's attempt at making his goal had been thwarted by a large chunk of flightsuit that had bound up in his well-oiled zipper. Lieutenant Thorpe shook his head. "Go to life support and see if they can help you. I'll be waiting for the bus."

A few minutes later Rick, too, was waiting for the bus, his g-suit good as new with the help of a large set of pliers. Putting his zipper failure behind him, Rick climbed into the bus and looked out in awe over the rows and rows of sleek white jets.

These jets were the real thing. The T-37 had been fun, but the T-38 was the White Rocket, the jet the Thunderbirds had flown, the same jet NASA used as a chase plane for the Space Shuttles. Almost all the fighter pilots in the Air Force had cut their teeth on these same T-38s.

* * *

Unlike the T-37, the T-38 had no starter. To get the turbine rotating until light-off, the crew chief had to connect a hose to force air over the blades, essentially push-starting the jet. This made the starting procedure simple, at least for the pilot.

After he had started both engines, Rick accomplished the required flight control checks. Because the flight controls in the T-38 were hydraulically actuated and not directly linked to the stick, it was important that Rick check them for proper response. If the hydraulic lines were accidentally hooked up wrong—backwards, say—it could make for some interesting aircraft control problems.

The flight controls checked good. So did the T-38's other systems. With Lieutenant Thorpe's okay, Rick called ready to the control tower, closed and locked his canopy, and taxied onto Laughlin's long center runway.

Holding his position on the runway, Rick mentally recited what he was going to do. When cleared for takeoff, he would hold the brakes and run the engines up to full military power so he could check the instruments. If they were in limits, he would smoothly push both throttles over their afterburner detents as he released the brakes. With the throttles full forward, Rick would be commanding ignition of the jet's afterburners. The 4,000 gallons of fuel poured into the afterburner per hour would boost the T-38's thrust 50 percent to 12,000 pounds. Once airborne, Rick would take the engines out of afterburner. Otherwise, the fuel on board would last only about fifteen minutes.

"Cool Two Five, cleared for takeoff," called the tower.

Okay, Rick thought, here goes. After checking his engine instruments, he cautiously pushed the throttles into afterburner. The nozzle gauge swung open indicating a good light-off.

Rick had disengaged nosewheel steering prior to brake release. Now all he had to control the track of the wildly accelerating jet was his rudder. And even though he did so with the rudder pedals at his feet, the job was a handful.

The next few seconds were critical. Until Rick reached his pre-calculated critical engine-failure speed, he could safely abort takeoff and stop within the remaining runway. After reaching that speed, if one of his engines failed, he was committed to taking the jet to the air—unless he wanted to end up in the barrier, a steel cable strung a foot above the runway for just such situations.

When he saw 135 knots on the airspeed indicator, Rick pulled back gently on the stick. The long slender nose rose from the runway. Fifteen knots later they were airborne.

Rick reached for the gear handle with his left hand and lifted the one-inch wagon wheel. Next he raised the flap lever. Both the flaps and the gear had to be up by the time they reached 240 knots.

Rick glanced down at the airspeed indicator. They were already at 230 knots. Wow! Rick pulled back on the stick to increase the climb and slow the jet. Instantly, the vertical velocity indicator was pegged at its maximum of 6,000 feet per minute. What a jet!

As he canceled afterburner, one engine at a time, Rick marveled at the T-38's sensitivity—his simulator rides and academic training hadn't fully prepared him for the feel of the jet. From the books Rick knew that full stick deflection would command two complete revolutions of the aircraft every second. But that was just a number. Actually commanding that kind of response was something different altogether.

The difficulties of controlling the sensitive jet were compounded by the T-38's other main attribute—speed. FAA regulations dictated a maximum airspeed of 250 knots for turbine aircraft flying below 10,000 feet. The T-38, however, like many military fighter and fighter-type aircraft, had a special waiver to 300 knots. Things happened fast at five miles a minute.

Actually, at the rate the White Rocket climbed, they weren't below 10,000 feet for long. Before Rick knew it they were passing 15,000, then 18,000, then screaming right through their assigned level-off altitude of 20,000 feet. Lieutenant Thorpe grabbed the stick in the backseat, taking control of the aircraft. He rolled it over on its back at 22,000 feet and pulled it down to the correct altitude. "You have to remember to lead the level-off by a thousand feet or so," he said as he gave the jet back to Rick.

After a quick level-off check to make sure that the oxygen regulators, fuel pumps, and cabin pressurization systems were working properly, Rick called for clearance to one of the "Ranch" practice areas. These areas were much like the "Ski" areas they had used in the T-37, except they were north of Laughlin instead of south and were about twice as big—both vertically and laterally.

Once he started doing acrobatics, Rick realized why the areas had to be twice as big. In the Tweet, he had started loops at 200 knots and could complete them within a 2,500-foot altitude block. In the T-38, he started them at 500 knots and used 10,000 feet of altitude—almost two miles.

After a full round of eye-watering acrobatics, Lieutenant Thorpe directed Rick through a series of traffic pattern stalls. This exercise taught Rick to recognize and recover from a situation where the airplane's angle of attack became so high that the airflow detached itself from the wing's surface.

The best indication of a stall was the feel of the aircraft. Because of its thin, symmetrical wing, instead of flying along fine and then suddenly stalling as it slowed, the T-38 stalled gradually, with an ever-increasing airframe buffet. As Lieutenant Thorpe described it, the buffet range started with the feel of mice running along the wings and increased to the feel of a whole herd of elephants stampeding out there just before the wing stalled. The key was to know just which animals were out there and how to properly handle them. Rick could do what he wanted with the mice, but he had to be nice to the elephants.

* * *

Once Lieutenant Thorpe was satisfied that Rick knew his zoology, he directed him to return to Laughlin for some touch-and-goes. The forty or so miles back to base didn't take long to cover, and soon Rick found himself face to face with one of the greatest challenges at UPT—bringing the White Rocket back down to earth.

Rick's first attempt was a straight-in approach to the center runway. Eight miles out and 2,000 feet above the ground, Rick extended his gear and flaps and slowed to the approach speed he had calculated to be 170 knots. Four miles out Rick started down the glidepath to the runway. Just as he had been taught, he was aiming for the center of the overrun, the thousand-foot stretch of concrete in front of the actual runway constructed to save planes and pilots from disasters of miscalculation.

Looking over the nose, Rick saw that the spot halfway into the overrun wasn't moving on his canopy. That meant a good aimpoint, just as Rick had learned in the simulator. He continued.

In the backseat, Lieutenant Thorpe strained to see around Rick's head. "Looking good," Lieutenant Thorpe coached. "Just keep bringing 'er down. Remember to aim for the center of the overrun. The flare should put you a thousand feet or so down the runway."

The runway was coming up awfully quick.

A quarter mile out Rick was still a little high, so he pulled both throttles back to idle, expecting the jet to float like the T-37 had during the flare.

They weren't in a T-37.

The instant the power reached idle, the jet began to sink. Lieutenant Thorpe shoved both throttles forward to stop the descent. But it was too late. With a *thunk* the jet hit smack dab in the middle of the overrun. Rick grimaced. His first landing in the T-38. Not too impressive.

Thanks to the overrun, however, nothing was broken. So, shaking off the mistake, Rick pulled up and to the left into the overhead visual pattern of Laughlin's outside runway. There Rick flew touch-and-go after touch-and-go. Each one gave him a progressively better feel for the mice on the wings and the runway under the nose.

With 1,200 pounds of fuel left, Rick called for the full stop. On this pattern, Lieutenant Thorpe decided to see how Rick would do with no coaching. Rick overbanked, but corrected. He got fast, but slowed back down. He pulled the power too soon, but put it back in. The touchdown was less than graceful, but he did it himself.

Yet, during the taxi back to parking, Rick wasn't thinking about how he had landed the jet by himself. He was thinking about landing in the overrun and making mistakes on virtually every pattern. He was also trying to remember where the heck all the switches were supposed to be positioned. He didn't feel proud. He felt overwhelmed and ignorant—until he taxied by the little Tweet waiting to get out on the ramp. Suddenly Rick forgot all about the things he didn't know and all the mistakes he had made.

With casual bravado he reached up to disconnect his oxygen mask, letting it hang rakishly to one side of his helmet. Then, as he taxied past the Tweet, Rick lifted his arm, which he had been resting nonchalantly on the canopy rail, and gave a wave to the student pilot looking up at him. Rick may not have mastered the White Rocket yet, but at least he was in it.

CHAPTER XII

Wings

I want wings, I want wings.
I'll get those gosh darn things.

— Post-it note, UPT student's refrigerator

B<small>Y THE TIME</small> R<small>ICK FINISHED</small> the navigation phase of pilot training
and could glimpse his wings just around the corner, he had
already received two notices from the Life Support shop to wash
his g-suit. The notices didn't come right out and say "wash your
g-suit." They were just photocopies of the proper laundry procedures for sanitary care of the government-issued *Anti-g Gar-
ment, Cutaway, CSU-13B/P*. Still, Rick got the hint. But he didn't
heed it.

Rick didn't wash the g-suit because he considered the crusty
white salt stain that was building up on the outside of the suit
to be good luck. To him it represented the experience he had
acquired in the summer heat of flying the T-38. It reminded him
of the lessons he had learned on his solo rides, his cross-coun-
try rides, and his supersonic run. It reminded him of passing his
contact check, his formation check, and his navigation check.

It reminded him, too, of the day he watched his friend Brian
Kephart bring a crippled T-38 in to land with one engine stuck
in full power and every caution light on the panel blinking in
random sequence. Brian, a former Air Force Academy line-
backer, had brought the malfunctioning jet in fast to the center

runway. Touching down long and unable to retard the out-of-control throttle, he tried to slow the airplane by holding the nose off the runway in an aerobrake. This caused the jet to become airborne again with one throttle in idle. Ten feet above the runway the wings stalled and the jet rolled into ninety degrees of bank. Miraculously, Brian was able to level the jet before it hit the ground. He engaged the emergency barrier at 150 knots, stopping just short of the overrun, with both motors still running.

Rick had landed just before Brian took the barrier, and he watched the whole scene from the taxiway. Rick could hear his friend's breathing as he keyed the mike just before contacting the thick steel wire. Up until that point, Rick had experienced only one kind of fear: fear of failure—fear of being unskilled, unable, incapable of making the cut. Though Brian had emerged unscathed, his experience had introduced a whole new kind of fear. One that could not easily be washed away.

* * *

The bulk of the rides Rick had flown during the summer had been formation rides. Though formation flying had been introduced in the T-37, it was in the T-38 that the students really had to prove their mettle and their potential to fly fighters.

As challenging as formation flying could be, Rick loved it. He loved it because it was fun. He loved it because it was legal. He loved it because it was graded.

He loved it because he was good at it.

Rick really couldn't put his finger on why formation came so easily for him. Maybe it was because of the "formation flying" he had done in the Champ. One day John had decided he would like to make a movie featuring Rick and him in the Champ flying formation with Matt in a rented biplane. John had titled the film "MARSA the Movie" in honor of the term for Military Accepts Responsibility for Separation. In it, John tried to put on film his theory that instead of buying thousands of multi-million dollar planes, the Air Force should buy millions of multi-thousand dollar planes. Planes that farmers could fly off their fields. Planes that didn't require pilots with perfect eyesight. After several weeks of practice and a couple of airsick amateur camera crews, they had abandoned the idea of submitting the movie to the Air Force. They had, however, compiled some pretty good footage and some pretty good experience.

More likely, though, Rick's formation abilities stemmed from the way he thought about flying. One day he explained it to Greg. "I try not to think about it at all," he said. "The real key is to keep in mind that all you're doing is flying relative to the other aircraft. If it banks up and starts falling out of the sky, you don't have to think about how much it is falling. All you have to do is match its movements. If you do that, you end up falling out of the sky at the same rate and it'll all work out. If you think about what you're doing too much, you lose the magic."

Rick knew this from experience. He had lost the magic for a frightening few seconds on his first T-38 solo-on-the-wing ride, a syllabus sortie designed to instill confidence in the solo student and terror in the instructor leading the flight—not to mention developing quite a salt stain by the end of the day.

Rick was coming home from the practice area, saddled up smoothly in fingertip formation on Lieutenant Thorpe's right wing, when it happened. This is great, Rick thought as he looked out at the jet just a few feet from him. I wish I could do this. Then it struck him. Hey, I am doing this. Suddenly, the question became, how am I doing this?

Rick's breathing quickened. He must have been watching an Air Force recruiting film in college and somehow dozed off. Now he was part of the movie—in a helmet and flightsuit piloting an Air Force jet.

As Rick tried to gain control of the unfamiliar craft, he saw the other jet begin to fly erratically, porpoising up and down.

Rick had to use full power to catch up. Rick surged ahead. He jerked the power back to idle.

Rick felt like calling out "Cut!" to let somebody know that there must have been some kind of mistake, that he shouldn't be in this movie, that the action had to stop. But before he could utter a sound, the memory of the last months came over him.

He hadn't been watching a movie. He had been learning to be a jet pilot at Air Force pilot training. He had spent hundreds of hours preparing to be in this position. He knew what to do. Falling back on this training, Rick took his left hand completely off the throttle and loosened his death-grip on the stick in his right hand. His actions had the intended effect. Instantly, the other jet settled out and came back into position. And it stayed there—not just for the rest of the flight, but for the rest of Rick's career.

* * *

During the summer, formation flying in the T-38 had become a part of Rick. Not just fingertip formation, but all formation. Formation takeoffs. Formation landings. Tactical formation, flown a mile out and line abreast from lead. Close Trail, fifty feet behind and ten feet below. Extended Trail, a 3,000-foot game of follow the leader where Rick used all his knowledge of aerodynamics, geometry, and gravity to stay behind his instructor in the other jet.

Rick couldn't explain well how to do it, but he sure *could* do it. In the air it was obvious to him. He was always there.

* * *

By the time Drop Night rolled around—one month before graduation—Rick had established himself as one of the top pilots in the class. He had worked hard to develop his flying skills, and he was proud of his achievements. For the Active Duty members in the class, however, class ranking went well beyond a question of pride. On Drop Night, class ranking determined the order in which they would choose their assignments.

Guard students were exempt from the worries of Drop Night. Those destined for tankers or transports already had their assignments. All they had to do was graduate. Those destined for fighters already had their assignments, too, as long as they obtained a *fighter* rating from their flight commander. Greg, Bud, and Rick had all been given this nod after outstanding performances on their formation checkrides. So, on September 25, they were relaxed. As were the Portu-guys. Their fate would be determined at a different Drop Night on a different continent.

In the classes before 92-01, Drop Night assignments had been determined by the wing commander with input from the flight commander and instructors. Working from the dream sheets turned in by the students, the commander would take the available assignments and dole them out as he saw fit. In that process, two things were certain: not everyone would leave the room happy, and everyone would leave with an assignment. By the time the Modern Day Cowboys came to Drop Night, the end of the Cold War and the subsequent reduction in cockpits available to pilots forced a new element into the assignment process—"banked" pilots who, after walking across the stage and receiving their wings, would be assigned to desk jobs while they waited for their turns in the sky.

The new system had another significant change: Assignments weren't given out; they were chosen, UPT-wide, via speaker-phone conference call with the other UPT bases. Two days before Drop Night, the Modern Day Cowboys received a sheet listing the aircraft that would be available to them. The students had two days to study the sheet and rank their choices. On Drop Night, when it came time for them to pick, they would stand up and choose from whatever aircraft were left.

* * *

The entire draft for class 92-01 lasted only twenty minutes. Buck Shawhan, picking first, chose an F-15 to Bitburg, Germany. Karen Policano opted for a KC-10 to Seymour-Johnson. Brian Kephart took a C-21 to Colorado Springs. Jeff Cantrell got a C-130 to Little Rock. It could land in the dirt, but it also had a place to put a coffee mug.

When it came his turn to pick, Tony Krawietz froze up. Having expected that all assignments would be gone before he got to choose, he hadn't made a list. Tony had miscalculated. There still remained a C-141 to Charleston, South Carolina, or a C-5 to Dover, Delaware.

The silence was almost unbearable as ears throughout Air Training Command strained to hear Tony's decision. Unable to stand it anymore, Greg leaned over and whispered something into Tony's ear, something about a weekend he had spent once in Delaware. Something that had nothing to do with airplanes.

"I'll take a C-5 to Dover," Tony declared.

"Laughlin chooses line forty-six," the moderator repeated, "C-5, Dover, Delaware."

When all was said and done, only half of class 92-01 would be going on to flying assignments. Half the people who the Air Force had just trained to be the best pilots in the world were going to walk across that stage at graduation, receive their wings, and wait two years to again take to the air.

For those who were going off to fly, the end of UPT marked the beginning of their dream of flight; for those destined for the desk, graduation marked the push of a giant *pause* button.

* * *

At the graduation ceremony, the Modern Day Cowboys sat in the two front rows decked out in military mess dress tuxedos complete but for silver wings. In back of the auditorium sat the members of class 93-01, all gazing admiringly at the students they were replacing, wondering to themselves if they had what it would take to find themselves up on the stage in a year.

The graduation speaker was Colonel Frank "Scrappy" McEwen, retired P-38 fighter ace. "In World War II," he told the class, "all we had to find the enemy were our eyes. Today's fighter pilots have technology on their side. They have radar, radios, ground controllers, missiles, and infrared detectors.

"But never think it's the technology doing the fighting. We are fortunate to have the most sophisticated Air Force in the world. But it's not the computers and electronics and advanced aerodynamic designs that make ours the most powerful Air Force on earth. It's the people behind these machines. In battle, it's the people flying them. It's their courage and their skill. Starting tonight, it will be your courage. Your skill.

"You are taking your places in the long line of aviators who have defended this country," he concluded. "You have sacrificed greatly and worked tirelessly to pass the test set before you. You have succeeded. Congratulations."

And with that, the Modern Day Cowboys filed on stage and pinned on their wings.

* * *

After the graduation ceremony, the pilots moved outside the auditorium and stood together beneath the clear Texas sky. Rick shook the hands of friends with whom he had just spent the best and worst year of his life. He shook hands with instructors, calling them now by their first names. He shook hands with his father and hugged his mother.

All around him, Rick heard words of praise, saw faces full of pride. Rick wanted to take part in these exchanges, yet somewhere in the midst of the congratulations, he found himself turning from the praise to face instead the rows of jets parked silently on the ramp.

There, in the moonlight, were the T-37s and T-38s around which his every thought had revolved for the past twelve months. Alongside the jets, Rick could see the wings he now wore on his chest and the salt-stained g-suit he had left hanging in the squadron building. He heard the deep roar of afterburners lighting for his first flight in the T-38. He felt the cold water of the Pogo Pool after his first solo. And he caught the scent of a brand-new Nomex flightsuit enveloping his body for the first time.

Rick felt a jumble of emotions. Relief. Exhilaration. Pride. Disbelief.

And something else, a feeling he couldn't quite put his finger on. Just a question he wanted to ask about what was to be required of him in return for his gift of wings. But on that night, the air was too filled with words of praise to hold up such a question, and he didn't even know whom to ask.

So Rick just touched the wings on his chest, smiled, and looked to the sky.

CHAPTER XIII

Holloman

It's not being a fighter pilot that's dangerous.
It's trying to act like one.

— LTC Mark Johnson

As Rick had progressed through Air Force training, he had lost
friends along the way. He had vied for his slot at Duluth with
fifty other applicants; he was the one who had been selected.
He had started flight screening with a class of twenty—he was
one of the sixteen who succeeded. Of his class of forty at AMS,
six candidates had been sent home without commissions. And
finally, the day they walked across the stage at UPT, only twenty-
one of the original thirty-one Modern Day Cowboys had earned
their wings. Some had washed out for academics, others for
airsickness. Most simply had not been able to keep up with the
ever-increasing demands of the flying program.

These were not people who had been chosen randomly off
the street. These were people who had already been screened
mentally, physically, and psychologically through the finest system of tests ever developed. Thankfully, both Rick and Greg
had somehow made it through these tests and found themselves
at Holloman Air Force Base in New Mexico to learn to be fighter
pilots. They were in the big leagues now—and they awoke each
day expecting the ax to fall.

* * *

On the day they in-processed at Holloman, Greg gave Rick a ride in his truck from their billeting rooms to the squadron building. As they approached the building they could see a row of the AT-38s they would be flying. It was a thrilling sight. The AT-38s had the same airframe as the T-38s they had flown at Laughlin, but the Holloman jets had been modified with gun cameras and bomb racks. Yet it wasn't these modifications that grabbed Rick's eye; it was the paint scheme. These weren't the solid white T-38s of student pilots. They were the camouflaged blue and white AT-38s of fighter pilots.

Ever since he had seen one of these jets on the ramp at Laughlin, Rick had been enthralled by the legend of the AT-38 "Smurf" jet. It was said that, because of all the aggressive flying done in the jets, the frames were bent and twisted out of alignment. Some, rumor had it, had been stretched a full six inches.

Putting these jets behind them, Greg pulled up at the large brick squadron building and parked the truck. He and Rick jumped out and entered the building. Inside, they found a small sign directing them down the hall to classroom B2. Following the arrow on the sign, they walked the long hall, mesmerized by photo after photo of fighter planes from every era of the Air Force.

Once they found the classroom, Rick and Greg took two empty seats and joined the other twelve officers in the room. Of these, eight were pilots and four were Weapons Systems Operators assigned to the two-seat F-15E Strike Eagle. Of the eight pilots, four were active duty OV-10 Bronco drivers in transition from the slow observation plane to the F-15. The rest were Guard Guys. One would be going to an F-16 air-to-ground unit. The other three, Scott Verville from Jacksonville, Hank Harder from Burlington, and Scott "Slim" Mulgrew from Atlantic City, would be going to air-to-air F-16 training with Greg and Rick at Kingsley Field in Oregon.

Soon after Rick and Greg were seated, Major Scott Fontaine entered the room. Major Fontaine was the officer responsible for training at Holloman. As such, he decided to set the mood right up front.

"Welcome to Holloman," he began. "I hope you're here to work, especially those of you who might have slipped by the screening process at UPT. This is no slouch program. In the last six months, we've washed out five pilots." He paused as he looked around the room. "They were all sent to Flying Evaluation Boards."

Mentally, the new pilots in the room reached up to hold a hand over the wings they had worked so hard to earn. They all knew that the Flying Evaluation Board was the courtroom for pilots. None of them knew exactly what went on behind the closed doors of such a board, but they all knew one thing: All pilots who walked into a Flying Evaluation Board had wings; not all pilots who walked out could say the same.

Having delivered his cheerful greeting, Major Fontaine began the routine in-processing paperwork, explaining what was in store for the students as they turned in their flying and medical records. In addition to two introductory formation training flights, three offensive rides, three defensive rides, and one final review ride, they would receive Basic Fighter Maneuver (BFM) academics, physiology academics, and a ride in the centrifuge.

With the mood set and paperwork completed, Major Fontaine dismissed the class members to begin their training for the centrifuge.

* * *

Before riding the "spin dry," the students received extensive academics on the physical demands placed on fighter pilots in a high-g arena. They learned once again how, when a high-speed fighter made a tight turn, centrifugal force pressed the pilot against the seat, drawing blood into the legs and away from the head where its oxygen was needed to nourish the brain. They learned how the eyes needed slightly more blood pressure to operate than the brain, so they could expect their vision to turn gray or even black just before they lost consciousness. Most important, they learned how to fight back by straining their muscles against their g-suits to keep the blood from pooling.

They had experienced g's already in the T-37 and even more in the T-38. In those jets, however, the only g's they felt had been the five or six that came when pulling through the bottoms of acrobatic maneuvers like loops or cloverleafs. In the F-16 and in the centrifuge, Rick and Greg would be enduring up to nine g's.

Because of this, their instructor had one final thing to say before he released the class for the day. "You're going to be riding the centrifuge tomorrow," he said. "Like we've been talking about all day, pulling g's can be very demanding. The centrifuge is no exception. In fact, sometimes it's worse than the jet, so treat tonight like a night before a flight. Go have a nice meal, get plenty of sleep, and whatever you do, don't go out drinking beer all night. You'll regret it in the morning if you do."

"I don't know what he was talking about," Greg said to Rick as the two of them crawled into Greg's truck. "Everybody knows a beer or two is good for pulling g's. He even said in lecture that it's good to be overweight and out of shape to get that extra-high blood pressure to take the g. There's nothing better for that than beer."

As strange as it sounded, Rick knew there was more than a little bit of truth to what Greg was saying. In the forties and fifties, back when the Air Force first came into being, the common wisdom was that small, thin, fit pilots could best stand up to the rigors of flight. As time went on and as airplanes were built to withstand and maintain higher and higher g-loads, all this changed. Extensive physiological research showed that the ideal physical makeup of a fighter pilot called for a short and stocky being who had a lot of muscle mass, some fat, and slightly high blood pressure. Fitness was essential—in fact, most fighter pilots engaged in intensive weight training—but excessive aerobic conditioning was shown to be detrimental to g-tolerance. Nobody ever accused Greg of being excessively fit, and in many ways it seemed that his lifestyle, if not his body, might indeed make him a g-monster. Still, Rick thought Greg had missed the point of the lecture and told him so.

"I don't think you should drink any beer tonight," Rick said. "Remember, twelve hours from bottle to throttle."

Greg shook his head. "First of all," he argued, "we're not flying tomorrow; we're just riding. And besides, it's not 'twelve hours bottle to throttle,' it's 'you can't smoke twelve hours before flying; you can't drink within fifty feet of an airplane.' Or is it the other way around? I can never remember. Anyway, I'm going to go grab a beer or two tonight and check out the town."

* * *

The next morning Greg arrived at the centrifuge with blood-shot eyes and a huge cup of coffee. By the time he got there, five pilots had already gone through the g-profile and had been debriefed about their performance of the g-straining maneuver. One debrief had been particularly lengthy because the pilot had relaxed his legs too soon and had lost consciousness under eight g's. He would be back to try again.

Rick arrived well ahead of his scheduled ride because he wanted to watch the others. As he climbed into the seat in the gondola at the end of the centrifuge's arm, he was wishing he hadn't seen what they had gone through. Now all he could think about was the image that had been in his mind as he had watched from the observation room: the small machine he had used to spin test tubes in high school science class. Rick had always been amazed at how fast that machine had turned. Now he was inside such a machine—a human specimen under the Air Force microscope.

Moments later, when the fifty-foot arm had spun up to its maximum rpm and his body was crushed against the seat, Rick had another concern—staying conscious.

Rick knew the ride would last only a few seconds, but under nine g's it seemed like he was in some kind of time warp. Rick's face pulled down over his chin. It became very difficult to breathe. He felt the blood draining from his head. He felt sleepy.

Yet somehow Rick didn't fall asleep. By straining his legs, his arms, and his stomach muscles, he managed to keep the blood up in his head, feeding his brain with vital oxygen.

Finally the centrifuge spun to a stop. Once still, the aluminum door opened automatically, and two technicians helped Rick out of his chair and onto the floor. Unable to balance himself, he reached for the wall to stabilize his world. For some reason, he had a sudden craving for cotton candy or a sno-cone.

As Rick stood there waiting for his head to stop spinning, he watched Greg finish off the last of his coffee and pop a dip of Copenhagen into his mouth. "See you boys in a little while," he said as he crawled into the mechanism's small cabin.

The class members in the waiting room glued their eyes to the video monitor displaying Greg inside his capsule. They were concerned about the big cowboy's ability to withstand the g's. They also wanted to watch him throw up.

The tension mounted as Greg ran through the nine-g profile. At seven g's, his entire neck and face swelled up until he looked like he was going to explode. At nine g's, Rick could have sworn that Greg's head had doubled its normal size.

Greg grunted and groaned. He wheezed and strained. He accidentally swallowed his tobacco. But he didn't black out, and he didn't throw up.

Rick was amazed. Greg had made it all the way through nine g's with one of the best resting g-tolerances the flight surgeon had ever seen.

Maybe there was something to the cowboy lifestyle after all.

* * *

The centrifuge was a good training aid. It allowed the students to experience a high-g environment with no real danger. In the centrifuge they could perfect their g-strain techniques without having to think about anything else.

They wouldn't have that luxury in the air. Out in the airspace over New Mexico they wouldn't have time to think about a proper g-strain. They would be too busy trying to survive against a threat behind them or working to threaten a jet in front of them that would soon be a threat behind them if they didn't properly manage their g's.

It didn't take long for Rick to comprehend the irony these g-forces brought to aerial warfare. All he had to do was consider a fight between an American F-16 and a Russian MiG-29. Both were multi-million dollar, state-of-the-art examples of each country's technology. Both had computers and radars and advanced engines—all placed in the hands of the best-trained fighters in the history of the world. Yet the fight would not necessarily be won through technological advantage. Maybe it would be won through superior physical stamina. Which pilot could handle more g's? Which pilot could fly better with all the blood rushing out of his head? It was back to survival of the fittest.

This was the philosophy that Colonel Frank "Strokes" Stokes brought to the class. The other instructors at Holloman were Air Force fighter pilots brought in from operational squadrons to share their experience. Colonel Stokes, who had retired from the Air Force after twenty-five years and three kills in Vietnam, was a civilian contracted by the Air Force to teach fighter fundamentals.

"There are two types of aircraft," Colonel Stokes told the class the first day. "There are fighters and there are targets. I'm gonna teach you how to be a fighter and how to make targets out of everybody else.

"Now," he continued, looking around the classroom, "how many of you enjoyed pulling nine g's in the centrifuge?" Not a hand went up. "How many of you have bruises on your legs from the seat?" All of them but Thielman raised their hands.

Stokes eyed the class warily. "Get used to it. Flying a fighter can be painful. It's the greatest thing in the world, but to do it right, it's gonna hurt. Believe me," he said fingering a long, ugly scar running up the side of his neck, "nothing hurts worse than doing it wrong." Rick winced.

* * *

For the next three weeks, Colonel Stokes taught the principles of one-on-one, air-to-air combat. He taught the high yo-yo, the low yo-yo, and the quarter plane. He taught how to track with the gun and how to survive against it. He taught with his hands. He taught with wooden airplanes on long wooden sticks.

Most of the instruction centered on the use of the gun. Colonel Stokes called this the fighter pilot's weapon of choice. He explained that the gun was honored with this distinction for two reasons.

The practical advantage of the gun over other offensive weapons was that it could not be defeated with technology. A semi-active missile like the AIM-7 Sparrow relied on radar signal guidance to find its target. If those signals were jammed electronically, the missile could be defeated. Likewise, flares ejected out of a defensive aircraft could confuse and defeat the seeker head of the AIM-9 Sidewinder heat-seeking missile.

More important to Colonel Stokes was the fact that to gun an opponent was to have utterly outflown him. A gun kill was a true fighter pilot's victory. Unlike employing a more advanced and much more expensive air-to-air missile, tracking with the gun had little to do with technology but a great deal to do with skill.

As fighter pilots, their job was to kill the enemy quickly and efficiently. If they couldn't get the kill right away, they had to work to maintain an offensive position until they could move in. If they couldn't get the kill at all, then they had to figure out some way of disengaging in order to live to fight another day.

Colonel Stokes explained early on that if they became defensive, their only hope of surviving against the gun was to cash in all their energy at the exact instant they thought their opponent was ready to pull the trigger, and keep jinking until their enemy ran out of bullets. "Jinking usually only buys a little time," concluded Colonel Stokes. "We'll teach you how to do it and how to do it well. But it's not a position you want to be in. If you're jinking in combat, you've already made a big mistake."

* * *

During the five weeks of Holloman, Rick made his fair share of mistakes. In class it all seemed so easy. When Colonel Stokes waved those sticks in the air, Rick was inspired by the clarity of the theory. In practice, with his oxygen mask pulled off his nose because of the g's and his IP in the backseat screaming at him for every error, nothing seemed clear.

Offense was quite similar to extended trail back at UPT, except that at UPT the leader had always tried to make it easy to stay in position. At Holloman the leader maneuvered so that Rick couldn't get into position—couldn't pull his nose on the target to release that lethal burst of gun camera film. And if it ever looked like Rick was getting to a guns solution, the lead jet would jink at just the right second and spoil the shot.

Defense was even harder. Once Rick heard the "fight's on" call from the offensive jet perched four or five thousand feet behind him, he had to twist in his seat and look over his shoulder while laying on six g's. Then he had to try to keep track of the offender as he fought to stay conscious while struggling to maintain the proper airspeed, proper lift vector, and proper altitude within the training airspace.

If he did fly through the floor—the prebriefed altitude simulating the ground—he would be declared "dead." If he slowed below his optimum corner airspeed and lost energy, he would soon be filled with imaginary bullets. If he pulled less than the maximum g's, it wouldn't be long before he would hear the kill word. If he pulled more than the maximum allowable g's, he might not be called dead, but he would have to call "knock it off" himself and get a structural check to make sure he hadn't broken the jet.

* * *

Because of the extensive use of afterburner, the Basic Fighter Maneuver (BFM) missions at Holloman usually lasted less than an hour. However, with briefing, flying, and debriefing, four or five hours could be devoted to the sortie. At least an hour was required to brief the sortie. During this flight briefing, the students were responsible not only for the familiar "EP of the Day," but also for the "Threat of the Day" which could be anything from an enemy aircraft to an enemy missile, gun, or radar.

After testing the students' knowledge, the instructors briefed the Desired Learning Objectives (DLOs) of the flight. At FISH-POT these DLOs had consisted mainly of taking off and landing safely. At UPT they had included flying good formation and making smooth instrument approaches. At Holloman, because they were now learning to be fighter pilots, these basic flying skills were taken for granted. No longer was simply flying the jet enough. Now they had to fight in it. The DLOs at Holloman were energy management, gunsight placement, and lift vector control. The requirement of perfect formation flying didn't go away. It was just that it was no longer a learning objective. It was just part of the job.

Holloman debriefs could last as long as two or three hours. First, the instructors asked if there was anything they could have done to have made the flight go better. In the history of Holloman, no student ever responded in the affirmative to this question. So, following a respectful interval of silence—usually a second or so—the instructors would step through the departure and recovery, hammering the students unmercifully on taxi spacing, rejoins out of traffic, and poorly flown formation.

After the instructors finished berating the students for terrible performance on departure and recovery, they would turn to the meat of the mission, the BFM. The worst thing about debriefing the BFM was that, as students, neither Rick nor Greg nor anyone else in their class could ever remember exactly what had happened during the set-ups. Partly because of the lack of blood in their brains and partly because it probably hadn't been all that clear in the air, by the time the students had landed, parked, and collapsed into their seats in the debriefing room, the whole mission was one giant blur.

The IPs, working off cards drawn up during the fight and their own mystical Situational Awareness (SA), remembered every turn, every reposition, and every shot. Using this information, they would draw up the fight on the board with a whole host of colored dry-erase markers in cryptic fighter pilot code.

They would talk about lead pursuit, lag pursuit, high yo-yos, and jinks. They would talk about energy states, altitudes, and lift vectors. Invariably, though, they would stop, point at a particular spot on the board, and ask that most dreaded question: "So, lieutenant, what were you thinking here?"

The students all hated this question. They hated it because they never had any idea what they had been thinking there. They knew they had just flown because they had fresh sweat stains on their flightsuits. Other than that, the sortie was usually nothing more nor less than a swirl of jets.

They could always remember clearly how hard it had been to breathe while pulling g's, and they could remember vaguely the yelling from the backseat. But what had they been thinking at that point in the fight? Probably, they had been thinking that flying defensive BFM was the hardest thing they had ever done and that they would rather roll out and die than turn another circle with a bandit they had lost sight of anyway. However, sensing somehow that saying this in the debrief would not be good for their careers, the students usually just fell back on the standard, "I thought that the bandit was stuck in lag, so I just kept my turn going."

"Well," Rick and his classmates got used to hearing, "you were wrong. I got a perfect guns track on you. You should have been jinking." They would all just close their lips and nod.

It was these head nods that got the class through Holloman. They became drinking ducks. Only they were better than ducks. Because if ducks were sitting at a debrief being berated for mistakes they could barely remember, ducks couldn't say "yes, sir" while bobbing their heads up and down. So, better than ducks, they sat there nodding, saying "yes, sir," and soaking up abuse and information.

* * *

As he packed up his truck for their departure, Greg summed up the Holloman experience. "You know, Rick," he said, sliding the ten-page review of his performance behind his seat, "when we walked across the stage at Laughlin, I thought I had the thing licked. I figured I could fly at least as good as any of the instructors. We get here and I feel like I can't fly at all. These here things say that we demonstrated 'average pilot capabilities and will require a great deal of attention to achieve the skill level required to fly the F-16 in follow-on training.' This makes me feel like I ain't even safe to drive this truck anymore!"

Greg's frustration was typical of the feelings of students departing Holloman. But he should have considered a couple of things. For one, he had never been safe to drive his truck, even back in Montana. Another was that his and Rick's reviews were among the best given that year.

And besides, Holloman was over, they still had their wings, and they were going to Oregon to fly F-16s.

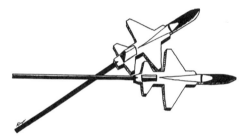

CHAPTER XIV

The Viper

*Mbr is ordered to perform active
duty (USC 505). Mbr will attend F-16
Operational TNG CRSE, Air Defense
Course, Kingsley Field...*

— F-16 Training Orders

AFTER SUFFERING THE TRIALS of Holloman, Greg and Rick took to
Oregon's Kingsley Field like pilgrims to the promised land. Like
the pioneers before them, the two had endured their share of
hardships and tribulations on the long trail west. But Rick's and
Greg's reward wasn't free land or gold. It was a treasure far
more precious—the F-16.

Before crossing into the land of milk and honey, Rick and
Greg had had to clear some enormous obstacles. There had been
AMS, FISHPOT, UPT, Holloman—and then, between Holloman
and Kingsley, Spokane's Fairchild Air Force Base for Survival
School where they learned to resist torture, patch up simple
leg fractures, and live on nothing but worms, snails, and snakes.

Compared to Fairchild, Kingsley Field was indeed paradise.
Nestled in the mountains on a high plateau of farmland deep
within the wooded peaks of southern Oregon, Kingsley was
just a few miles south of the small city of Klamath Falls. Mount
Shasta loomed only sixty miles south of town. Awe-inspiring
Crater Lake National Park lay just an hour's drive north. The

only thing Rick and Greg found wrong with the area was that, after graduation in six months, they would have to leave it.

Kingsley started life as a Naval Air Station in World War II. After the war the field was converted back to civilian use. In 1975 it re-opened as an interceptor base for the old Air Defense Command. In 1984 the Air National Guard took over Kingsley and turned it into a training base for Air Defense Fighters as the active duty Air Force was gradually phased out of the Air Defense role. Kingsley really came into prominence when, on October 1, 1991, the last active duty interceptor squadron came off Alert, and full responsibility for Continental Air Defense was placed squarely on the shoulders of the Air National Guard.

Initially, the Air Defense units had been equipped primarily with the F-4D Phantom II, the enormous 1950s-vintage twin-engine fighter. Commensurate with their expanding responsibilities, the units gradually made the transition to the specially modified Air Defense F-16—a single-engine, single-seat fighter in the Mach 2 speed class, widely regarded as the greatest dog-fighter ever designed. The Air Force named this awesome machine the Fighting Falcon. Its pilots called it the Viper.

Yet it wasn't just the jet or the mountains that Rick and Greg liked so much about Kingsley. It was the learning environment. At Kingsley they were surrounded by instructors who had but one goal in mind: to train them to be the best fighter pilots in the world. The instructors weren't there to screen, harass, intimidate, or eliminate. They weren't there to motivate or initiate the students into some kind of close-knit fraternity. They were there to teach the pilots to take their places along the wall of American Air Defense.

Drawing on the combined experience of exceptional instructors from the Air Force, the Navy, and the Marines, Kingsley had put together an instructor force second to none. The instructors logged time in the greatest flying machine ever to rule the sky. And they did it in the Guard, where they could fly for their entire careers without fear of staff tours or desk jobs.

* * *

By the time Greg and Rick arrived at Kingsley Squadron Operations on their first day, Slim Mulgrew, Hank Harder, and Scott Verville were already waiting in the main briefing room. Rick and Greg walked in and took their seats next to their old Holloman friends, swapping stories of their latest adventures.

Outside the open door, Rick could see four students engaged in a game of "combat" foosball, a game which, in order to tune fighter pilot reflexes, was played with three balls at the same time.

At exactly eight o'clock, Major Paul "P-Squared" Prange walked into the classroom. The students began to rise to attention. P-Squared waved them down. "Keep your seats," he said. "Welcome to Kingsley. I'm Paul Prange, and I'm in charge of academics.

"We think we have an exceptional training program here at Kingsley. I hope you'll think so, too. You're going to find that things are a little different here than at your other training bases. You're going to be learning to fly the F-16 ADF, Air Defense Fighter. The ADF is a special jet. It's got an ID light, electronic interrogation capability and is modified to carry the AIM-7 Sparrow radar guided missiles.

"The ADF is an F-16 like no other. And the F-16 is like no jet you've ever flown. It's no trainer. It's a fighter. A twenty-million-dollar weapon entrusted to you by the American taxpayer.

"Think about that for a minute. Twenty million dollars. That single jet represents the combined lifetime economic output of a whole bunch of people. And you're going to be at the controls. All alone. That's a lot of responsibility. And don't think for a second that we aren't going to dock your pay if you wreck one." Greg's face contorted slightly as he tried to work the F-16's price tag against his lieutenant's pay.

For the next fifteen minutes, P-Squared continued his introduction as he collected the students' paperwork and passed out information packets about Klamath Falls.

"The course is broken up into five phases," he explained. "The first is the conversion phase, where we teach you the basics of flying the F-16. That part is easy. Anyone can fly a fighter. What we're really here for is to teach you to be fighter pilots. We'll start this process with Basic Intercepts and Basic Fighter Maneuvers. Once you get those down we'll teach you Advanced Intercepts. In the last phase we will combine all these skills in Dissimilar Air Combat Training against either F-15s or F-18s."

Each member of the small class smiled. They couldn't help it. They were all thinking about fighting F-15s.

P-squared read their minds. "Before you can think about fighting," he concluded, "you have to know how to start the jet. To get you going on that, I'd like to introduce you to a special tool we have created here at Kingsley. Its name is Computer Based Instruction Testing Service, C-BITS for short, and for the next few weeks you're going to be seeing quite a lot of one another." With that he led them out of the briefing room, past a long hallway hung with pictures of classes who had gone before them, and into a room full of office cubicles and computer screens.

* * *

From the C-BITS interactive computer screen, Rick and his friends learned everything from the theory of fly-by-wire flight to procedures for locking up a target and shooting it with an AIM-7 radar missile. After each lesson the computer tested them on what they had learned.

For two weeks, Greg, Slim, Hank, Scott, and Rick spent twelve hours a day with their eyes fixed to the computer screens.

Occasionally, students from the senior class would pop over to the terminals to ask how the new students were doing. Overwhelmed by photo-electrons, Rick and the others usually just looked up with bloodshot eyes and murmured that they were doing fine.

They were lying, of course. None of them felt that he was doing fine. Each felt that there was absolutely no possible way he was going to remember all the information this electronic firehose was trying to force into his head.

At UPT they had essentially memorized the Dash-1s for the T-37 and T-38. At first, that, too, had seemed impossible. But after hours and hours of study, they had been able to master every word.

The T-38 Dash-1 was three-quarters of an inch thick. The F-16 Dash-1 was three inches thick.

To make matters worse, the Dash-1 itself was only a small part of the F-16 documentation. In addition to T.O. 1F-16A-1 there was T.O. 1F-16A-1 Supplemental, of equal bulk. There was also T.O. 1F-16A-34, the non-nuclear weapons delivery manual for the jet. Heaped on this were all the tactics manuals, intelligence information, and Air Force and North American Aerospace Defense (NORAD) intercept regulations. This made for a formidable stack of reading. And quite a headache at the end of the day. C-BITS reduced this workload somewhat by condensing these reference manuals, but the load of information was still overwhelming.

The only thing that made the studying bearable was the sound of jets flying in the pattern overhead. This, combined with the time they were spending in the simulator, reminded the students they were learning numbers, concepts, and procedures not for an academic quiz, but in order to fly the F-16.

* * *

Rick's first chance to put into practice what he had learned came three weeks after he arrived in Oregon. Waking up to sunshine streaming into the bedroom window of the haunted farmhouse he and Greg had rented, Rick jumped out of bed, threw on the cleanest flightsuit he could find on the floor, and hurried down to the big farm kitchen. Being a little short on time before brief, he mixed up a fighter pilot breakfast for the road: half a pot of cold coffee, two eggs, and four scoops of Joe Weider's Dynamic Muscle Builder. This he poured into a half-full quart of milk and mixed it with a few hearty shakes. A blender would have worked better, he knew, but this way he'd have some chunks to chew on while he drove to work.

Rick pulled on his boots, ran a razor over his face, grabbed his breakfast, and jumped in his station wagon for the five-mile drive to base.

After Rick arrived on base and sat through his preflight briefing, he walked to the life-support room, grabbed his helmet, and put on his g-suit. Because the F-16's ejection seat had a built-in parachute, he didn't have to wear one on his back. Instead, he wore a lightweight harness that would connect him to the seat. Thus equipped for flight, Rick walked out to the ramp, inspected the jet, and strapped in.

In the back seat of Rick's two-seat, B-model F-16 that day was Captain Kirk "Skull" Bartlow, a former active duty instructor with well over 2,000 hours in the F-16.

As the crew chief came up the ladder to help him with his harness, Rick reviewed the mission data card on which he had written the specifics of the day's sortie. After takeoff they'd fly out to Goose Military Operations Area (MOA) for some acrobatics and handling exercises. Then they'd come back to the field and practice some landings. Following three rides like this, he would fly solo in single-seat A-models for the rest of the course.

To get the engine going in the F-16, all Rick had to do was flip a switch and move the throttle to idle. The starting procedures didn't end there, however.

Probably the most important task was programming the Inertial Navigation System (INS), the magic multi-axis gyros that would constantly compute the jet's location during the flight—without any input from electronic transmitters on the ground. The INS would tell him where he was and, with the help of the computers, where he was going and how to get there.

Rick entered his navigational points through the data entry keyboard on the Fire Computer Navigation Panel (FCNP), his interface with the F-16's onboard computer. He could also have entered his waypoints into a data transfer cartridge on a personal computer in the squadron and then loaded the cartridge directly into the F-16's computer. Either way, once the computer knew this navigational information, it could tell him which heading to fly and what airspeed to hold to reach each point right on time.

Much of this INS data was accessible to Rick on the Heads Up Display (HUD), a three-quarter-inch thick piece of glass mounted above the instrument panel in his line-of-sight out the front of the cockpit. The computer projected green images onto the glass from below. A small video camera transferred both the image and the view out of the front of the jet to a video tape recorder stashed in the F-16's belly.

The HUD could display airspeed, groundspeed, altitude above sea level, altitude above ground level, vertical velocity, steering bars, weapons parameters, and lead computing gunsights. It could also display a Flight Path Marker which would indicate exactly where the jet was going, taking into account g-load and wind drift.

The F-16 INS and HUD together delivered a feature that allowed even the biggest hamfist to fly a great instrument approach. Pilots called this feature Herm. On the HUD, Herm first appeared as a small circle about one third the size of the Flight Path Marker. Until the plane approached the glidepath, Herm just sort of sat there. Then, as the plane reached the glidepath, Herm would sprout a tail. All Rick had to do was center the flight path marker over Herm and follow him down a perfect instrument approach path.

The inherent danger in all the fineries of the INS and computer wizardry, Rick reminded himself, was the temptation to rely on it without backing it up with the good "steam gauges" laid out on the instrument panel. Like anything, the INS could fail. It could just up and die, or worse, it could start spitting out incorrect information. If he followed the wrong path, he could find himself augured into the side of a mountain—not something he wanted to experience, particularly on his first flight as a Viper Driver.

* * *

After he made sure he had completed all the engine start steps on his checklist, Rick called for taxi instructions from the civilian tower. "Kingsley Ground, Skull One taxi one F-16 IFR with information India."

"Skull One," the ground controller replied, "Taxi to runway one-four, wind one-two-zero at ten."

Taxiing the F-16 was unlike taxiing any other jet Rick had flown. He didn't have to hold the nosewheel steering button to gain control of the nosewheel. This meant he didn't have to use his hands at all during the taxi. That made it easy to wave to civilian passersby. He also couldn't rest his arms along the canopy rails. Regulations prohibited taxiing with the canopy open. In fact, he had to close the bird-strike-proof bubble canopy prior to engine start to preclude the enormous engine from sucking loose items—like checklists, pencils, and pilots—from the cockpit and down into the intake.

Before taking the runway, Rick pulled the jet into the end-of-runway arm/de-arm area for a "last chance" inspection. The purpose of the end-of-runway inspection was twofold. First, it gave ground crews a chance to look the jet over one last time to make sure it hadn't developed any leaks or other problems since engine start. Second, it allowed any live ordnance to be armed away from the populated area of the ramp. Though Rick would fly only two missions at Kingsley with a live gun and would never carry live missiles, every sortie required the arming of the chaff and flare dispensers at the rear of the jet.

Another part of "last chance" was the Emergency Power Unit (EPU) check. Because the F-16 had only one engine, it also had an EPU designed to activate immediately in the event of engine failure to power the flight control computers and hydraulics long enough to get the jet down safely. Although he wouldn't be winning any national soaring titles in the F-16, if the engine quit, Rick could glide approximately seven miles for every 5,000 feet he descended. If he lost the engine at 20,000 feet, for instance, he could glide twenty-eight miles before hitting the ground, or, he would hope, before making a successful emergency landing.

After Rick got the green light indicating the EPU was operating properly, he gave the crew chief a thumbs up, armed his ejection seat, and called ready for takeoff.

"Skull One," the tower replied, "cleared for takeoff, runway One Four, turn left on course, climb and maintain one five thousand, contact departure two five five point niner."

Checking to see that the area behind him was clear, Rick pushed forward on the throttle and guided the Viper into position on the runway. Holding the brakes, Rick pushed the power up to 80 percent rpm. The engine roared behind him as he checked the instruments monitoring its operation. Everything looked good as Rick released the brakes and smoothly moved the throttle up to full military power, which in the F-16 provided enough thrust for takeoff. Under normal operations there was no need to use the afterburner.

The jet accelerated. Within seconds Rick was at 70 knots, clicking off the nosewheel steering. At the predetermined rotation speed of 140 knots, Rick pulled back gently on the stick.

It didn't move!

And yet, as if by thought command, the Viper lifted from the runway. Accelerating through 170 knots Rick reached up with his left hand and raised the landing gear handle. Had he been in a T-38, Rick would have been reaching for the flaps at about that time. But there was no flap lever to contend with in the F-16. In fact, there were no flaps. The whole trailing edge of the wing acted as a computer-controlled aileron and flap at the same time. This surface was called a flaperon. All leading-edge flap and flaperon movements were controlled automatically by the flight control computers for maximum performance.

By the time the gear came up, Rick was in love with the strange immobile side-stick controller that connected him to the jet. It made it seem that the jet was a part of him. Or that he was a part of it. Whichever, it was wonderful.

What a difference this was from the Champ. Moving the rusted old cables connecting the Champ's stick to its control surfaces had always been something of a chore. Rick had had to physically pull the airplane through the air.

But not the Viper. Rick thought about banking left, and the jet banked left. Rick thought about climbing, and the jet climbed. It wasn't just the plane that was flying; it was Rick.

True to its name, the side-stick controller wasn't between Rick's legs, but on his right side. Rather than resting his arm on his right leg, he set his arm in a cradle that jutted out from the right interior of the cockpit.

The stick in the T-37 had been a simple lever connected through cables directly to the control surfaces. Slightly more complicated, the stick in the T-38 operated hydraulic valves that moved the control surfaces an amount proportional to the stick movement. The stick Rick now held in the Viper was not mechanically linked to the control surfaces in any way. It was merely a pressure transducer that sensed the pressure from his hand and converted it to electrical inputs that were fed to the computer. It was the computer that decided how to move the control surfaces.

The flight control computer on the F-16 was not introduced just so engineers could move the stick over to the side. Without the computers controlling the stabilators, flaperons, and rudder, the jet would depart controlled flight in less than a second.

This instability had actually been designed into the jet. By placing the F-16's center of gravity very close to its center of lift, the engineers had created a jet with wings and horizontal stabilizers that produced lift in the same direction, with no unnecessary drag. In the F-16 the pilot didn't have to increase negative lift in a turn—just decrease the lift on the horizontal stabilizer. The result was a highly efficient high-g turn and an aircraft so unstable that no human pilot could ever fly it by hand.

* * *

This turn performance became obvious to Rick out in the Goose MOA twenty miles east of Kingsley. Within the area's confines, Rick spent fifteen minutes practicing turns, acrobatics, and nose-high recoveries.

The turns watered Rick's eyes. All he had to do was roll into ninety degrees of bank and give a tug on the stick. *Wham*, nine g's.

Nine g's was the most Rick would ever get out of the F-16. Even if he tried pulling on the stick with all his might, the computer would step in and say to itself: "Hey, this guy is pulling back on the stick with fifty-eight pounds of force. Of course, I don't recognize anything over thirty-two pounds, but at least I know that he must really want to turn hard, the way he's pulling. I'd really like to make him happy. Heck, at this airspeed I have enough energy for fifteen g's easy. But wait, the most g's my programmers said that I could pull is nine so I don't damage my airframe. I know just how much to move the horizontal slabs for nine g's at this airspeed, so here goes." *Wham,* Rick would be a 1,500-pound pilot squashed in his seat, out of breath, and glad his g-suit was inflating to keep some of his now-heavy blood out of his legs.

Though it was impossible to over-g the jet, it was still very possible to over-g the pilot. A couple of weeks before Rick had arrived at Kingsley, a student in the class ahead of him passed out on a BFM sortie.

The student had been in full afterburner driving to the turn circle to get to his IP's vulnerable cone. As he reached the turn circle with nearly 500 knots on the jet, he reefed back on the stick. Five seconds later the jet was nosing down toward the earth and gaining airspeed. The student was asleep.

When he awoke a few seconds later, he realized that he needed to recover immediately. Pulling back on the stick to recover from the vertical dive, he lost consciousness again. This time, however, he fell asleep with the nose of the F-16 pointing straight up, so he awoke with plenty of altitude to recover. The HUD camera recorded the entire episode.

Rick and his classmates had listened to the story and watched the tape in rapt, attentive silence. They knew it could just as well have been any one of them.

* * *

By the time Rick got back to the pattern, he had forgotten he was operating a machine. He wasn't sitting in his jet; he was wearing it. He didn't actuate controls; he thought and the jet moved. In fact, with his head and shoulders separated from the air only by the bubble canopy, it didn't even seem there was an airplane around him at all. It wasn't a machine; it was part of him, a natural extension of his self, enabling him to attain speeds and perform maneuvers that would have been sheer fantasy in any other plane he had flown.

Flying up initial, Rick tried to take all this into account for the touch-and-go. At the breakpoint, Rick imagined himself rolling into ninety degrees of left bank. Without really feeling it, his hand applied left pressure on the stick; they were in the pitch. Rolling out parallel to the runway, Rick reached up with his left hand and lowered the gear lever. Approaching the perch point Rick extended the speedbrakes and made his gear-down call.

"Skull One, base, gear, touch-and-go," Rick said.

"Skull One, cleared touch-and-go," the tower replied.

Staring at the angle of attack "staple" now present in the HUD, Rick imagined the descending turn he wanted the jet to take. As if by magic, the jet followed this path through the minute pressures of his hand. By short final Rick had the thing wired. The staple indicated exactly eleven degrees. The flightpath marker was planted exactly on the threshold just as Skull had told him.

About halfway through the overrun, Skull, speaking for one of the first times from the back seat, told him to add a little power. He complied, easing back on the stick slightly at the same time to shift the flightpath marker to the far end of the runway. This was the most difficult part of landing the jet because the flight control computers were biased for nose rate, not nose position. By pulling on the stick, Rick was really telling the computer to move the nose up a little faster, not a little higher.

Not that Rick was thinking of rate bias. He was thinking of keeping the jet below the maximum fifteen units angle of attack. The jet would fly at higher angles of attack, but above fifteen units the afterburner nozzle and the speedbrakes would scrape on the runway during landing.

Just prior to when he thought they would be touching down, Rick pulled the power to idle and began to flare like he had in the T-38. As he had always done in the T-38, Rick pulled slightly back to hold the jet up. It didn't work. The wheels touched down and before he knew it they had bounced ten feet in the air.

Skull chuckled in the back seat. "You've got to be careful not to flare too much," he laughed. "At eleven units the jet still wants to fly. You need to actually let off on the backstick pressure right before you touch down. Otherwise you'll end up bouncing every time."

"Yes sir," Rick replied, his body surging with excitement as he pushed up the throttle to go around for another touch-and-go.

Skull was an excellent instructor, so it didn't surprise Rick that he was right about his prediction of Rick's landings: he did, in fact, bounce every time. However, with each landing the amplitude of the bounce decreased, until finally, on his full stop, Rick settled down with a hop barely perceptible from the ground.

* * *

Back on the ramp, Skull and Rick unstrapped from the jet and walked over to the debrief building to turn in the maintenance forms for the jet. At the desk, the crew chiefs asked Rick how many touch-and-goes he intended to log on his first landing. Everyone laughed.

Rick, remembering the bounces, laughed, too. But as he left the room and walked back out on the flightline, his thoughts turned toward a more profound implication of the day's sortie. As the years had progressed, flying had steadily occupied more and more of his life. What at first had been just a part-time diversion had turned into a full-time occupation. Until that first ride in the F-16, however, Rick had always felt that if flying were taken away, his life would continue on happily in other directions. But as he walked past the rows of Vipers highlighted against the mountains in the distance, he knew that this belief no longer applied. Rick had found his dream. And now there was no letting go.

CHAPTER XV

Trapper's

Do not ask how strong your enemy is.
Ask instead where you can find him.

— Creed of the Russian Fighter Pilot

THE GREATEST DANGER IN being a new Viper driver was the way the early training combined student ignorance with fighter pilot ego. By the time Rick and Greg soloed the single-seat A-model F-16, they had only scratched the surface of what they needed to know to effectively fly the jet. Nevertheless, because they woke each morning knowing they would be spending the day flying fighters, they both thought most highly of themselves.

To bring these two forces into a safe equilibrium, Kingsley had long ago set aside an institution of extraordinary power. It wasn't C-BITS. It wasn't the commander's office. It was a place where more theories had been expounded, more lessons learned, and more egos tamed than in all its classrooms and supervisory offices combined. It was called Trapper's Inn, the Kingsley All Ranks Club.

At Trapper's, with a crowd comprised almost entirely of pilots and other squadron personnel in the know, there was no hiding from the blunders of the day.

Trapper's was also a place of learning. Following a particularly long debrief, or sometimes *instead* of a particularly long debrief, the students would often wander the two blocks from the squadron building to Trapper's to sit and talk for hours. About airplanes. With their hands.

* * *

The last time Greg and Rick sat at Trapper's was representative of its place in their training and in their lives.

It was the Friday of their final week of flying, and the two friends were ready to unwind after a long day at work. Holding the door open for Greg to enter behind him, Rick was struck, as always, by the sharp contrast between the bright sunshine outside of Trapper's and the utter darkness inside. It was as if all the light from the world was being absorbed by the dark paneling that lined the club. Not waiting for his eyes to adjust, Rick followed as Greg dead-reckoned his way to the bar, taking soundings, Rick imagined, from the banjo player picking away in a corner of the room.

At the bar, Greg saddled up to the corner stool that in the past weeks had been acknowledged as his own. Rick grabbed the one next to him. Kathy the bartender brought them a pitcher of beer and three glasses. "Here you go," she said.

"Thanks, Kathy," Greg drawled as he took the pitcher and filled up two glasses, handing one to Rick. The third he kept empty, not for some unexpected guest but because he needed a place to spit.

By this time, Rick's eyes had adjusted enough to make out his now familiar surroundings. Off to his right was a small dining area. If he had turned around, he would have seen three or four tables with chairs, a dartboard, and a jukebox. In the corner was the banjo player, whom Rick now recognized as Lieutenant Colonel Dick "Shadow" Houkes, the chief radar controller at Kingsley. He was being joined by Major Johnny Adkisson, who was pulling a well-worn guitar from a battered case. A doorway at the far end of the bar led to a large pool table. Across the main room from the musicians was the long bar, its wooden rails worn smooth by countless elbows. On all the walls hung pictures of the friendly adversaries who had fought against Kingsley students.

Rick felt a brush on his arm. It was Doc Berini, the Kingsley flight surgeon. The flight doc pulled up another stool, got a glass from Kathy, and helped himself from Greg's pitcher. "Well, boys," he asked, "what do you say?"

"Well, Doc," Greg replied, quaffing his first draught of beer. "All I can say is I'm turning out to be a great fighter pilot."

The flight surgeon laughed. "I suppose you guys can't do what you do unless you think you're the greatest." He paused. "It's kind of like being a doctor. But in my job I worry that by my mistake somebody will die, while I live. And you guys—you live in fear that by your mistake your enemy will live, and you'll be the one to die."

"I guess you're right about that," Rick replied, "except for one thing. In Air Defense if you make a mistake, it's not just you who will die, but those on the ground you are flying to protect."

"And you're wrong about something else, too," Greg inserted. "Fighter pilots don't live in fear."

At these words, the memory of his last ride in the two-seat trainer flashed into Rick's mind. On that ride Rick had done something he *had* feared. At least at the time. He had refueled in the air.

As he had rolled out a mile behind the flying gas station, Rick was amazed at the size of the tanker. He was used to doing rejoins on T-38s. Compared to them, the KC-135 was absolutely enormous.

Stabilizing in trail, Rick ran through the pre-refueling checklist. The most important step on the list called for him to open the refueling door on the top of the jet just behind the canopy. Looking down to make sure he had hold of the correct switch, he moved it to the outboard *open* position and waited for the blue *ready* light to appear next to the HUD.

"Skull One," Rick called over the radio, "precontact, stable ready." Because he had never refueled before, he also added the obligatory "Skull One is a first-time student."

Rick could imagine the groans inside the big aircraft as the boom operator replied. "Skull One, cleared contact."

The move to the contact position was the moment of truth. Skull had taught him to drive slowly, straight at the boom, and to trust the boomer to swing the boom off to the side, flying its two small wings with control sticks from his observation perch in the back of the tanker. Rick tried to relax, but all he could think about were the stories he had heard about booms coming through canopies.

As he moved slowly under the tanker's tail he looked for the director lights they had studied in class. Situated in two parallel rows along the bottom of the KC-135, the director lights told him how to move the jet to stay in position during the refueling. Before contact with the boom, the boomer operated the lights by hand, commanding him to move forward or back, up or down. After contact, the lights automatically displayed positioning commands.

Once he had some experience, Rick rarely used the lights during daylight refueling. Instead, he positioned the jet according to his own set of visual references. Of course, if all else failed, there was always the signal he used on the way to gaining that experience that first day—the boomer's excited voice on the radio calling "back three, down two, down three. Breakaway!"

* * *

Greg laughed as Rick mentioned the anxiety he had felt on that first refueling ride. "Hah," Greg said, "refueling is a piece of cake."

Rick jumped in to defend himself. "I'm not saying I'm still scared of it. I was just a little nervous that first time. I think it's great now. You get to stay up and fight a lot longer."

"Yeah," Greg added, "it lets you stay up a lot longer, sometimes longer than you want, eh, Spraygun?"

Greg got him good with this one. Spraygun was a call sign Rick hated, not because of the name itself, but because, like all good tactical call signs, it had been inflicted upon him as a direct result of aerial buffoonery. Frankly, Rick wished to forget the name and the incident that had inspired it. Knowing this, Greg took advantage of the moment to relate the entire story to Doc Berini.

As Greg had implied, because aerial refueling greatly extended a plane's range and time aloft, it also led to some of the most impressive aerial maneuvering of all—relieving oneself in a single-seat fighter. When the crew members of an aircraft like a KC-135 tanker heard the call of nature, all they had to do was get up from their seats and walk to the bathroom. In the Viper, however, it was a different story. Even if the pilot could get up, there'd be no place to go.

Rick learned this on one of his first intercept rides. An hour-and-a-half and two refuelings into the two-and-a-half hour mission, the four cups of coffee he had consumed during briefing started begging for attention. Realizing that it was much better to go when he would fill up only half of one of the special "piddle packs" instead of, say, one and a half piddle packs, Rick turned on the autopilot, unfastened his lap belt, and contorted his body into what he thought was the proper piddle pack position.

Rick leaned back in his seat, sighing with relief as he completed the job. When finished, he pulled up the small plastic pouch to seal it for disposal. To his horror, the bag was empty.

He had hoped to keep his poor aim a secret. But there was only so much one could hide from a crew chief.

* * *

By the time Greg had finished his detailed description of Rick's embarrassment, he, Rick, and Doc Berini were joined by their other class members—Slim Mulgrew, Hank Harder, and Scott Verville, and by one of their instructors, Major Eric "Yo" Bondshu.

What with the crowd, and in the spirit of Trapper's, Rick decided to take the offensive as he poured himself another beer.

"Well," Rick said, "at least I never did a weapons check on an airliner…"

Even as the words escaped Rick's mouth, he regretted their leaving. Perhaps he was going too far. After all, it could just as well have been he who had screwed up. But then again, it had been Greg; so what the heck, why not tell the story?

Greg's mistake had resulted from a simple lack of Situational Awareness (SA), that mystical attribute through which a fighter pilot synthesizes radio calls, radar information, audio tones, threat warning chirps, and visual cues into an understanding of the events happening around him. Without SA, a pilot could get himself in trouble. Without SA, a pilot could not win, regardless of the capabilities of his weapons. Without SA, a pilot could get killed.

Greg's lack of SA had involved the classic error among new fighter pilots—focusing on technology and ignoring the obvious. More specifically, Greg's mistake had involved something the great fighter pilots of World War II had never used. Greg's mistake had involved RADAR.

Back in the F-4, running the radar had been a kind of black magic. The F-4 system more or less just threw radar energy out into the air and collected the returns back into the antenna in its nose, leaving the Weapons Systems Operator in the back seat to sort out the information.

The F-16 didn't have a back seat, and it didn't have a Weapons Systems Operator. Instead, it had an extra fuel tank and a computer. The fuel was nice to have, but it was the computer that allowed the jet to be flown as a single-seat interceptor. Even though the computer couldn't read approach instructions with calm assurance when the pilot was low on fuel on a pitch-black night in a rainstorm, it could take raw radar returns and turn them into pictures and numbers that made sense.

The primary display of this information was the Radar Electrical Optical (REO) display between the pilot's legs, where the stick would have been on a conventional airplane. It displayed aircraft as far out as eighty miles. Once the radar locked onto a particular target, the REO displayed the target's airspeed, aspect and altitude.

Some radar information was on the HUD. With a radar lock-on, the HUD projected a green box over the target to help the pilot pick up the target visually. It also displayed weapons symbology for the missiles and a computer-controlled Lead Computing Optical Sight for the gun, which predicted the flight path of the bullets as they sped from the gun at the rate of 6,000 rounds per minute.

The controls for these weapons and the radar were on the stick and on the throttle. There were radio switches, gun controls, radar controls, missile select buttons, speedbrakes, and more. To get through Kingsley, the young pilots had to have more than just stick and rudder skills. They had to be able to play the piano, in ragtime, at nine g's.

On the particular ride Rick was describing, Greg had needed to tickle the ivories soon after takeoff. Too soon, as it turned out.

The departure was to be radar trail. Greg's instructor, Doug "Hammer" Dean, would take off first. Greg would use his radar to trail Hammer through the weather. As he lined up for takeoff, Greg looked down at the REO to set it up on a five-mile scope with a slight antenna uplook. With a start, he realized he hadn't yet turned the radar on.

He immediately, if tardily, turned the radar control switch to *Air*. The radar entered its self-test warm-up period. "I really ought to tell Hammer," he thought. But if he said something, then everyone listening on the radio would know he had messed up his checks. Maybe the radar would be ready before they were cleared for takeoff.

"Hammer One flight, cleared for takeoff," called the tower. Greg mentally coaxed the radar to hurry along in its self-test cycle. With a wave, Hammer released his brakes and accelerated down the runway. Greg looked down at the radar scope. It was still timing in.

Twenty seconds later the radar was still not on-line. But to maintain proper spacing Greg released his own brakes to follow Hammer, who had already entered into the base of the clouds.

A few moments after he entered the clouds himself, Greg's radar finished its self-test and began to function. Intent on hiding the fact that it had ever been off, Greg fumbled over the radar's controls, searching high and low for Hammer.

Bumping the radar out to a twenty-mile scope, Greg got a hit. He moved the cursor over the target and locked it up by depressing the designator button under his right thumb. "Hammer Two is tied," Greg called over the radio as he looked at the target data block that had come up on the REO. Hammer was on his nose for ten miles at an altitude of 30,000 feet. Greg was so relieved to have found his flightlead that it didn't even occur to him how strange it was that his flightlead had traveled that far and climbed that high in only twenty seconds.

To close the gap between him and Hammer, Greg lit the afterburner and pulled the jet into a thirty degree climb. Half a minute later he popped out of the weather at 20,000 feet. Staring through his HUD, Greg could just barely make out his objective, now six miles in front of him, through the target designator box on the HUD. "What good eyes," he thought, "to be able to see him from so far away."

"Hammer Two is visual," Greg called.

"Roger, cleared weapons check," Hammer answered.

Greg complied, selecting the gun and squeezing the trigger to make sure it was really safed. Next he ran his fingers through the automatic acquisition capability of the Air Combat Mode (ACM) of the F-16's radar. In ACM the radar looked out to a specific area of the sky and automatically locked the first thing within ten miles that it saw.

Greg then checked his Advanced Interrogator Friend or Foe (AIFF) system. When he hit the interrogator button any aircraft within his REO's field of view squawking the prebriefed or pre-loaded secret code would appear as a hollow square on his REO. If the aircraft he was locked to was squawking the proper code, the word *FRIEND* would appear in the HUD.

When Greg moved his right thumb outward to interrogate Hammer's mode three code, he didn't see *FRIEND*; he saw *UN-KNOWN*. This meant one of two things: either Hammer's transponder was malfunctioning or the airplane Greg was following wasn't Hammer at all.

There at Trapper's, Greg sure wished that the first explanation had been the right one. But it wasn't. In his hurry to catch his flightlead, Greg had missed him entirely. Instead, he had completed a weapons check on an airliner on its way to San Francisco, or Los Angeles, or who knows where, but definitely not on its way out to the practice area to teach him intercepts.

* * *

This was a pretty good story, and Rick was glad to tell it. But Greg still had one card to play in this land-based game of Ego Shootout at the Top Gun Corral.

"Oh, yeah," Greg said above the laughter, "I may have intercepted an airliner, but at least I didn't kill my flightlead."

Greg had him there. Two weeks before, during Dissimilar Air Combat Training (DACT), the summit of his aerial tutelage, Rick had committed fratricide, the most serious mistake a student, instructor, or combat fighter pilot could ever make.

He had been flying tactical formation on the wing of Captain Pete "Maggot" Bristol against a two-ship of Navy F-18 Hornets. Rick was flying this formation, a mile out from Maggot's right wing, so that he could maintain a visual lookout, to make sure that Maggot's *six* was clear. At pilot training, where he had learned to fly tactical formation, and even at Holloman, where he had learned to fight in tactical formation, the six had always been clear. In DACT, however, he really had to look out. Because, just maybe, a threatening aircraft would be sneaking up from behind.

Rick checked his radar, then looked left, dragging his visual scan across Maggot's small fighter and parking it a few miles behind his exhaust. There, closing fast, was an F-18.

"Maggot, break left, bandit six o'clock low, flares!" Rick called out over the VHF radio. He and Maggot both broke left. Foolishly, the F-18 kept turning toward Maggot, apparently not seeing Rick against the sun. This sandwiched the F-18 between the two of them.

As Rick pulled his nose around to point at the Hornet, he selected the ten by sixty auto acquisition mode on his radar. The jet's computer voice called out "lock, lock" indicating it had found the F-18. With the lock, the slaved seeker-head of Rick's AIM-9 heat-seeking missile was "growling" fiercely in his headset to let him know it "saw" the hot exhaust of the F-18. Rick pushed the "uncage" button on the throttle. The growl turned to a solid, steady tone. A solid self-track. Rick pushed the pickle button. The imaginary AIM-9 Sidewinder whooshed off the missile rail on the way to its real-life target.

Rick double-checked his HUD to make sure the shot was valid before calling the kill. He didn't want to have to pay the F-18 pilot the required five dollars if his HUD tape revealed an invalid kill during the debrief. After satisfying himself that there were no flares coming out of the Hornet and that the missile had been in parameters, Rick sang out over the common UHF frequency, "Maggot Two, Fox Two kill, single F-18 Angels twenty turning through north." The F-18 performed the obligatory aileron roll of death and descended below the combat floor.

Rick smiled inside his oxygen mask, thinking how lovely it was to be sitting in an F-16 calling a kill on an adversary. Six months ago he would not have imagined enjoying Air Combat Training. At Holloman, Air Combat Sorties had been some of the most stress-filled moments of his life. Something had changed. Maybe it was his confidence. Maybe it was his abilities. More likely, it was that in the F-16 he was all alone. He could take the fight one-circle or two-circle. He could take the fight low, take it high, or take it to the sun. He could pull to the g-limiter, sacrificing his Viper's energy to bring its nose around the circle for the first shot. Or he could hold the jet at corner velocity, hoping to win a sustained energy fight.

As aircraft commander of his single-seat fighter, Rick was free to make his own judgments and his own decisions—and follow them through to see if they were the right ones—to see if he would have lived or would have died.

Well, he had made the right decision this time, that was for sure. And it felt good. Five years ago he would not have been able to have imagined such a feeling. Five years ago he would have thought that such scenes took place only in the movies. But now it was no actor on the screen; it was he, Lieutenant Rick Wedan, in the skies of Oregon engaged in aerial combat as sophisticated as any the world had ever seen.

Rick's revelry was interrupted by a high-pitched chirping from his Radar Warning Receiver (RWR). Aircraft radar set off this receiver in the same way police radar set off automobile radar detectors. In fact, under some circumstances, the F-16 radar could actually set off automobile radar detectors. Rick knew this, because sometimes on his way back from the practice areas he would lock up cars racing down the desert mountain highways. When Rick first locked them up, the REO would often display their speed as ninety or one hundred miles per hour. Within seconds of the lock, however, the speed would drop down to a more moderate, and legal, fifty-five.

But at 20,000 feet it wasn't a state trooper's radar that was making Rick's pulse quicken. It was a Hornet that had locked him from behind. Rick broke hard into the signal.

"Maggot flight, break right, Two is spiked, right four o'clock." This was bad. With a radar lock, provided he was within range, the F-18 could launch an AIM-7 radar missile at Rick before he even knew where it was. Rick had to honor the radar spike and go on the defensive, trying to break the lock by turning ninety degrees to the radar warning indication and putting the F-18 "in the beam" with no relative motion between him and the ground. This would confuse the F-18's pulse doppler radar into thinking that Rick wasn't a jet but a piece of the earth.

By making him go to the beam to defend against the missile, the F-18 gained a desirable tactical position. Even if Rick could defeat the missile by breaking the Hornet's radar lock, all the time Rick was saving himself from the missile he wouldn't be fighting the F-18. Rick needed some help.

It came from Maggot, who had just picked up the F-18. "Maggot One is tally, visual, engaged," he called as the bandit reacted to his presence. "Two, come off west to re-enter." As directed, Rick turned west and pushed forward on the stick, to unload the g from the aircraft and pick up some airspeed.

Rick assessed his situation. Everything looked good. His radar spike had gone away, so the F-18 must be engaging Maggot. All Rick had to do was turn back and take a quick heater shot from below the fight. With this plan in mind, Rick pitched back in, ready for his second kill of the day.

He did not see what he expected. In fact, he did not see anything at all. No F-18, no F-16. Just sky and clouds and earth. Nothing looked right. He wasn't even sure he was still in the United States. Rick had no SA; he was *tumbleweed*. He'd have to make the call.

Then he saw something on the horizon. It looked like two fighters. Maybe he could salvage this after all.

In a flash, Rick pulled his nose around toward the jet Maggot was pushing around the turn circle. Selecting the *boresight* auto mode on the radar, Rick pointed at the dot and depressed the *designate* button to lock it up. The HUD indicated a perfect AIM-7 shot. Excited, Rick pushed the pickle button.

Immediately, his own radar warning receiver lit up. This, and a loud beep in his headset indicated that his Constant Wave (CW) energy generator was sending out a signal to guide his imaginary Sparrow missile. Rick ignored the RWR warning, hoping that his adversary would do the same, and watched the time of flight countdown for the kill. Four, three, two, one, zero. It had worked! "Maggot Two, Fox One kill, defensive F-18 angels sixteen passing through east."

Both F-18s were dead. Rick waited for the "knock-it-off" call from Maggot. It came one second later. Then Maggot added on the interflight frequency, "Maggot Two, why don't you interrogate the jet you just shot."

Rick moved his thumb to the interrogate position and looked up to the HUD. The word *FRIEND* appeared. Fiery knots flared in Rick's gut. He had just shot his instructor.

* * *

Fortunately, the AIM-7 Rick had fired at Maggot had existed only in his computer's algorithms and hadn't actually come off the

rail to kill his flightlead. Rick had bought Maggot a beer that
night at Trapper's and was glad for the chance to do it.

Rick was not so glad that Greg had just related the story in
such depth to the crowd of pilots. He wanted to retaliate. But,
his store of suitable comebacks exhausted, he instead fell back
on the fighter pilot standard: "Yeah, that was stupid—but I'd
take you any day."

Greg snorted. "You name the time and the place, and I'll be
there to gun you just like I did Snake yesterday when I started
defensive from a six thousand foot perch set-up…"

* * *

As Greg started to put down his glass so as to have two free
hands to recreate the fight of the day before, Rick found himself viewing the gathering as if standing in the cool darkness of
the late evening outside the window.

The banjo still played, the pool balls still cracked, but to
Rick all this was muffled. He saw only a group of young men
gathered around their common purpose, engrossed by the mo-
tions of one in their midst who was chasing his hands through
the air.

The scene had repeated itself thousands of times within the
hallowed walls of Trapper's. Multitudes of battles had been
fought, engagements reenacted, and planes and pilots lost—all
within the safe confines of the club.

After what could have been hours or minutes or years, it
occurred to Rick that there was no longer a crowd. No banjo.
No guitar. Just he and Greg, talking about what they had done,
or would do, or would have done.

"You know," Greg said as he dumped the last of the beer
into his glass, "we've all made our share of mistakes and had
our share of screw-ups. But I can tell you right now I'm ready

for what's out there. I'm not saying that I want war or anything, but I'm ready for it.

"I feel like a guy who has been practicing three-point shots for years. A guy who can make every basket. A guy who hopes he doesn't find he's wasted his life away throwing balls through a hoop nailed to a garage somewhere."

Rick nodded as Kathy turned down the lights. He understood. They had skilled themselves in a profession that had been put in place to prevent the need for such skills.

Rick also understood the irony of his own feelings about his profession. He had come to Kingsley because he loved to fly. Flying fighters—the best of the best—had seemed the culmination of that love. But he now recognized that there was another line that could be drawn to the Viper, one that Rick had gradually begun to see as he progressed through training. That line didn't start in an old cloth-covered airplane on some dirt strip in California. It started with the first spear, the first club, the first sword. It started with the first challenge, the first response, and ended not at a graceful flying machine, but at one of the most formidable weapons ever devised.

Rick searched himself for an understanding of where on these lines he now stood, how far along these lines he had traveled in the years since he had flown the Champ. He didn't want to kill, that was certain. But somewhere deep within him was the desire to fight, the need to prove himself. This was the essence, he now realized, of the feeling he had known on the night he pinned on his wings. Now a full-fledged fighter pilot, he wondered if, perhaps, this feeling wasn't really the cause of wars in the first place—not political, moral, or ideological differences, but things much more deeply rooted in man's existence.

Maybe he and Greg would sort this out sometime—but now was not the time, because the lights were dimming and Kathy was standing by the door waiting to usher them out. So, gathering their jackets, the two friends said good night, walked through the swinging door, and put Trapper's behind them.

CHAPTER XVI

Paradise Bar

Here dead lie we because we did not choose
To live and shame the land from which we sprung.
Life, to be sure, is nothing much to lose;
But young men think it is, and we were young.

— A.E. Housman

THE COWS GRAZED PEACEFULLY outside the screen porch of Ford's Cafe as Matt told Rick and Greg about Paradise Bar. Matt had just finished up Holloman and would be starting F-16 school the next week. He had made it to Klamath Falls just in time to see them graduate from Kingsley.

"So, tell me more about this Paradise Bar," Greg said, naturally intrigued by anything with such a name.

"Paradise Bar," said Matt, pausing in disgust as Greg spat the last of his Copenhagen through a large hole in the screen porch wall, "just happens to be the most famous airstrip in these parts. It's a grass strip in a canyon out by the coast. It's about a thousand feet long and boxed on three sides by hundred-foot cliffs. The only approach is through the canyon, and the only way to get to the strip is from the air or by boat."

"A thousand feet is a little short for a Viper," Rick said.

"Yeah," said Matt, "but it's nothing for a Champ."

"We don't have a Champ," Rick said.

"Ace does."

Matt was invoking the real-life legend, Ace Bigby, the crusty aviator for whom John had worked as a Fire Patrol Pilot. It was Ace's Champ that Matt and Rick had flown back in college. Rick sketched the stories for Greg.

"Yep," Matt said, "Ace's shop is just over the mountains about ten miles outside of Roseburg. John brought the Champ back when he moved up to Alaska to fly float planes. I bet Ace still has it there. And if he does I'm sure he'd let us take it to Paradise Bar if we promised to be real careful."

Something didn't feel right to Rick. "Wasn't Paradise Bar the place Ace wrecked the Champ in the first place?" he asked.

"No," replied Matt. "That's what I always thought, too. But it wasn't at Paradise Bar—it was on the *way* to Paradise Bar that he ran into trouble. John told me that Ace had been flying the Champ all summer off a hay field next to his hangar. When the hay was low, he could make it off no problem. By late summer, though, the hay was so high it had really slowed his takeoff roll. He wasn't going fast enough to lift off the ground and plowed the Champ through the fence at the end of the field, right into the church cemetery. That's where most of the damage came from. He went through the fence pretty clean, but the tombstones did a number on him."

Matt pressed his proposal. "So, what do you guys think? You're fighter pilots. Paradise Bar should be a piece of cake. C'mon. We've at least got to find out why they call it Paradise Bar."

That was enough for Greg. "I'm in," he said as he pushed his chair away from his syrup-filled plate, now devoid of pancakes. He looked to Rick. "Well, I guess it couldn't hurt," Rick said, though he knew better.

* * *

Once the three pilots got to Roseburg, they had no trouble finding the cemetery outside of town, and once they found that, they had no trouble finding Ace's place down by the river. Disguised as a shed, the shop was made primarily of corrugated tin craftily held together with a variety of other building materials and old airplane parts. On the side of the largest wall, in black spray paint, were the words: "Bigby Air—If It Flies, We Can Fix It."

Greg parked the truck outside the sliding gate. The three young men got out and ducked beneath the rusted barbed wire strung between the leaning wooden posts. What looked like a side door to the building was held shut with an old yellow-handled screwdriver shoved through a wire loop. Fearing that he might dislodge the door from its frame if he knocked, Matt led the way around the hangar to a larger door that swung open into the shop. There, his hands covered with glue and sawdust, stood a wild-eyed man of indeterminate age.

Emmit "Ace" Bigby had flown fifty missions over Germany during World War II. The P-51 Mustang pilot had six confirmed kills before his twentieth birthday. Everyone he flew with had figured he would end up as America's top ace. Then one day a bullet from one of the new German ME 262 jet fighters exploded in his canopy and left him blind in one eye.

He somehow hid the fact from the flight surgeon at his base in England for two weeks. Then one evening he was challenged to a game of darts by the base commander. Not only did he lose for the first time since arriving in England, but his blindness was discovered. Ace had been sent home a reluctant hero.

After all he had been through in the war, when he found himself back home and still alive, Ace had concluded that the rest of his life was just gravy. Resigning his commission, he started his own flying service. Each summer he battled the western blazes as a fire-bomber, always careful to conceal his ocular impairment. Winters he spent working on his airplanes. For fifty years, what letters he had sent all carried the same return address. And every aviator who had ever found his way to Ace's field had flown away better for the experience.

* * *

Hoping they hadn't startled him, Matt, Rick and Greg introduced themselves to the legend, finding themselves surreptitiously trying to determine which was his good eye.

"Well, good to see you guys," Ace said. "I remember John telling me about you. He's up in Alaska, now, you know."

"Yep, sure do; he's having a great time, too," answered Matt. He paused to study the nest of wooden shavings at Ace's feet. "Say, what are you working on?"

"Oh," replied Ace, "it's a Kragen-Hatfield. All wood with manually retracted gear. It's coming along pretty good, except the guy I got it from didn't even have enough pieces for me to make all the patterns I need."

"Don't you have plans?" Matt asked.

"Hell, no," replied Ace. "Nobody has plans for these things anymore."

"Well, then," Matt persisted, "how do you know if you're doing it right?"

"I don't," he replied with a grin, "But then again, neither does anybody else."

The sun was already high, so Matt figured he had better get down to business. "Ace," he said, "Rick, Greg, and I were having breakfast over at Ford's Cafe this morning and were wondering about—"

Ace broke Matt off with a wave of his hand. "Ford's Cafe! I haven't been there in years. Back when I was working out of Klamath we used to go there all the time. Does it still have all the old airplane pictures on the walls?" he asked.

"Sure does," answered Greg.

"—Paradise Bar," continued Matt. "We were talking about Paradise Bar."

Ace's eye sparkled. "Ahh, Paradise Bar. I've had some pretty good times there, that's for sure. Used to be popular. Just about every pilot on the West Coast came in at one time or another—back when people used to know how to fly taildraggers."

Ace chuckled. "I remember once back before the war when I was a kid. We were sittin' down there in the winter around a big potbellied stove. It was cold out. Bone cold. So we were staying inside pretty much. All of a sudden we hear engine noise. My uncle Walt goes to the door and looks out. He says it's a Stearman with one guy in the back hole. We were all thinking that the guy must be nuts flying in an open cockpit on a day like that. So we closed the door, figurin' we'd see him in a couple a minutes or so. Well, he come down all right, but twenty minutes after we heard him land he still hadn't come in. Walt and I went out to see what was goin' on. We found him there at the end of the runway sittin' in the plane with the engine off. We ran up to see inside the plane 'cause we thought he might be dead. When we get close we hear a voice from inside the cockpit. 'I'm frozen here, I can't get out.'

"Well, me and Walt jump up on the wing and lift this tiny old guy out of the cockpit and carry him back to the stove inside. He couldn't stand or even really sit, so we just laid him down in front of the stove and let him lie there like a dog in front of the fire. After a while, he thawed enough to take down a bowl of soup and stand up by himself. I remember we were all wondering what we were going to do with the guy when out of the blue he thanks us for the fire and opens the door to leave.

"My uncle asks, 'Are you sure you're okay?' The guy says, 'Yes sir, I'm fine. I'm on my way down to Georgia. It should be warm down there. But I wonder if I could ask you to help me into the cockpit.' Well, we hoisted him back up and threw over his radial engine for him. It started right up and a few minutes later he was gone. Migrating south, I guess."

"Ace, we want to go there," Greg blurted. "Do you think we could borrow your Champ?"

"I don't know," replied Ace. "That's one heck of a tough approach. I know you guys fly those fancy jets with all the computers and such, but Paradise Bar is something different altogether. Do you have any experience with this sort of thing?"

"Well," said Greg, "I guess I've had my fair share of experience with bars. We just want to find out what makes this one so special."

Ace smiled. "I don't think you quite understand. Paradise Bar isn't a saloon. It's a sandbar. It's just a small spit of land on the Deschutes River barely big enough to put a plane on. There's a shack there but it ain't much to look at, just a place to get in from the weather and warm yourself."

Greg was disappointed. Matt was inspired. "Ace," he said, "flying is what we do. It's who we are. Ever since we saw the Champ down in California, flying is all we've thought about. I can't tell you the number of classes I missed because the weather was nice and John called and needed a gas stooge for the Champ. All that time we heard about you and about flying into places like Paradise Bar. If we don't see it now, we may never get another chance."

Ace looked at Matt thoughtfully. After a few moments he said, "Well, I know what you're saying. I used to think the same way myself. Really, I guess the only thing I regret is that I can't go with you myself. Heck, it's been so long, I don't know that I could make it anymore, anyway. So I guess what I'm saying is that it's fine by me. Just head straight west until you get to the river you can't see across. Then you know you've gone too far. Turn around and fly about twenty miles. You can't miss it.

"Just be careful. Remember, you can only shoot the approach from the north. Pass east of the small hill and chop the power. You have to pull the power before you actually see the strip or it'll be too late, and once you pull the power you've got to land. With the cliff, there's no going around. So when you hit the ground, hit the brakes hard.

"But you don't have to worry about going off the end of the runway. There's a huge boulder at the south end. It'll stop you for sure."

"The Champ's out back behind the shed. It might need some gas. I've got a can here, and my felt hat's hanging there on the wall for straining gas if you've got some in your truck."

The young military pilots shook Ace's hand, thanking him profusely.

* * *

Rick followed Matt and Greg out behind the shed. There, resting awkwardly in grass grown tall under the Oregon summer sky, sat the Champ. It looked much more like a wreck than an airplane. It looked exactly as Rick remembered. It looked great.

Greg was the first to speak. "Where's the airplane?" he asked, staring straight at the Champ.

"You're looking at it," Rick said, remembering the first time he had seen this grand old multi-hued, cloth-covered taildragger.

Greg was incredulous. "You've got to be kidding," he said, reaching in his back pocket for some reassurance in his tin of Copenhagen. "This looks like a wreck."

"Yep," Matt returned, "ain't she beautiful?"

Greg made his way through the knee-high grass up to the airplane, cupping his hands to see through the window into the cockpit. Turning around he said, "Well, it's only got two seats. Since you guys have so much experience, why don't you take it. I'll wait here with Ace."

Matt explained. "Greg, it's only got two seats, but there's room for at least three. The tractor seats Ace put in are plenty wide." Then, in a spontaneous bit of fabrication that amazed even Rick, he added, "In college we sometimes flew with four."

"C'mon, Greg," Rick added. "It's relatively safe."

"I don't know," Greg said. "I've got my good jeans on."

Matt glared at him. "But, all right, I guess I'm in."

"Okay," Matt said, rubbing his hands. "Let's get her going."

* * *

It had been a long two years since his last Champ ride, but the knack of siphoning gas from a truck's unlocked gas tank and straining it for water through an old felt hat came back to Rick as if he had done it just the day before. So did hand-propping the tired old engine. Carefully, he positioned his feet on the tall slippery grass, pulling the prop through a few revolutions.

"Try it again!" Matt yelled out the open door. Rick reached up once more and grabbed the propeller with already sore hands.

Watching them from the doorway of his old workshed, one eye open and unseeing, the other narrowed keenly, stood Ace. A smile lit his haggard face.

It was the middle of September, and though the sun was bright in the southern Oregon sky, the autumn chill was setting in, and the long, thin steel was cold against his unprotected fingers. For the tenth time he threw the full weight of his twelve-year-old body into the prop, pulling the engine through its cycle while his uncle moved the throttle back and forth, hoping to find that one special position.

With a cough, the engine sputtered to life, and young Emmit instinctively backed away from the whirling propeller. Like a cat, he ran to the airplane door and jumped in the empty seat in front of his uncle. "Keep the stick back in your lap," his uncle called over the engine, which was now humming away in a low, solid rhythm. "Keep the tailwheel down so you can steer..."

Ace shook his head at the memory and looked out to the cemetery at the end of the field and at the three young men now taxiing across the field of hay, heading off to find adventure in the feel of smooth grass beneath their tires and the thrill of cloth-covered wings lifting them into the sky.

With a wave, he returned to his work.

CHAPTER XVII

Unknown Rider

Laughing through clouds, his milk-teeth still unshed,
Cities and men he smote from overhead.
His deaths delivered, he returned to play
Childlike, with childish things now put away.

— Rudyard Kipling, "R.A.F. (Aged Eighteen)"

FOUR MINUTES AND FORTY-EIGHT SECONDS EARLIER, Rick Wedan had been a twenty-four-year-old lieutenant half dozing in front of the Alert building's satellite-equipped, rear-projection big-screen television. Five years earlier, he had been a nineteen-year-old college student putting five dollars worth of gas into beat-up old gas cans in exchange for a few hours in the air. Now he was on his way to match himself against an intruder whose face he would never see.

By the time Rick's landing gear came up, the long orange stream of fire trailing Dave's airplane had disappeared completely in the clouds.

Rick searched his radar scope for Dave. Nothing. No, wait—there it was, an eighth-inch green square, two and a half miles up the scope, just where Dave's twenty-second head start should have put him.

Rick ran the acquisition symbols over the target, then locked it by depressing the designate button under his right thumb. The square turned to a diamond and Dave's altitude, airspeed and heading came up in the lower right corner of the scope. Two thousand feet and climbing. Four hundred knots. Heading three-one-zero, the runway heading. It looked like Dave, all right. Heeding lessons learned from Greg's airliner intercept, however, Rick moved the designate button outward to interrogate the classified mode four squawk to make certain it was Dave. The diamond turned hollow and the word *FRIEND* appeared in the HUD.

"Tundra Two tied," Rick called over the VHF radio.

"Copy tied," replied Dave. "Lead's coming left to one-six-zero, maintain five-mile trail."

"Two."

As Rick accelerated, he watched the diamond on his scope slide off to the left as Dave began his turn south. To increase his spacing to five miles, Rick let the diamond drift forty degrees left before beginning his turn to follow.

The tower directed them to switch to 253.4, Oakgrove's tactical control frequency.

"Tundra push two five three point four," Dave called.

Rick rotated the knob on his radio and switched it from the preset channels to the manual 253.4.

"Tundra check."

"Two."

"Oakgrove," Dave called, "Tundra flight passing five thousand for three-five-zero turning to one-six-zero."

"Oakgrove is radar contact, confirm weapons safe," Oakgrove answered.

Rick checked to make sure his master arm switch was in the down simulate position as Dave replied, "Tundra is noses cold."

"Oakgrove copies, bogey bears one-six-five for one hundred thirty miles, estimate low. Climb and maintain flight level three-five-zero vector one-four-five for cutoff."

Dave acknowledged the call and then, according to procedure, asked for authentication to be sure that he was really talking to Oakgrove and not an imposter who had come up on the frequency. "Oakgrove," he said, "authenticate Delta Echo."

Rick pulled out a package from his g-suit pocket and scanned the secret 2001 authenticator matrix, finding the "D" row and reading over to the "E" column. The letter was "P."

"Oakgrove authenticates Papa," replied the controller. Now they could rely on voice recognition for the rest of the intercept unless they were ordered to do something drastic, like arm their weapons.

As Dave leveled at 25,000 feet and stabilized at 400 knots, Rick broke the lock on his radar and ran the cursor out to an eighty-mile scope. Now he could search for the target. He would maintain trail using the unlocked hits on Dave's jet. If necessary, he could also use his interrogator to "paint" Dave's transponder reply.

Switching on the autopilot to maintain altitude and heading, Rick looked about his cockpit, checking one more time that he was strapped in and that all his systems were working properly. He was and they were. The engine instruments still looked good. His fuel tanks were feeding properly. Everything was fine.

With these checks complete and the autopilot controlling the jet, Rick was able to give some thought to the aircraft they were about to encounter. It looked to him like a drug runner. The target was flying low. That indicated someone trying to avoid radar detection. And it was flying at night, without a flight plan.

It was also slow. Oakgrove had said 200 knots in its *Unknown Rider* calls. Not real slow, but too slow for an airliner and not an impossible speed for a druggie light twin.

What were the other possibilities in the scenarios Rick had briefed when he had verified for Alert qualification? Russian

Bear bomber on a long-range mission to test America's air defense? Possible, but a little low and too slow.

Cruise missile launched from a bomber or ship? Maybe, but it was unlikely that the Air Defense radar could pick up such a small target that far out, and it was a little slow for a cruise missile.

How about a nontraditional cruise missile? Maybe an old DC-3 filled with explosives launched by terrorists and outfitted with a thousand-dollar guidance system from off-the-shelf Global Positioning Systems parts that could take it to almost any target in the United States. And what if the payload wasn't conventional explosives, but some kind of crude nuclear device? There was plenty of unaccounted-for fissionable material out there since the end of the Cold War.

Maybe a renegade fighter out of Cuba. Or maybe one launched by the Cuban Air Force. It was, after all, still a Communist country, and only a stone's throw from Florida. But why? Why would a country like Cuba ever threaten a country like the U.S.? It didn't make sense, that was sure. But then again, it didn't have to.

Dave's voice crackled over the radio, breaking Rick's thoughts. "Tundra Two," he called, "I've got a small problem up here. My radar just went black. I've recycled the power a couple times but I'm not having any luck. My interrogator is still working, though, so I can maintain trail. I'm spinning to the right. I'll climb above three-five-zero until I'm behind you. You have the lead."

I have the lead? Rick thought. I'm not a flightlead. I'm a wingman. I'm a lieutenant! I can't have the lead!

That is not what Rick said. He keyed the mike and replied, "Copy, Tundra Two has the lead." Rick sounded calm. He wasn't.

Dave wasn't offering Rick the chance to fly his homebuilt or make a landing at Wawa. Dave was telling him to lead a two-ship of F-16s at night against a target they hadn't even yet seen on radar.

What was he doing here? He had expected to be back at the Alert barn relaxing and getting accustomed to the Alert lifestyle. They were supposed to just spend their four days watching television and relaxing, maybe flying once or twice for practice, but not actually getting scrambled. Not for real. The most stressful part of Alert was supposed to be choosing what movie to watch—not getting the lead!

* * *

Drawing on his training, Rick regained his confidence. It's just like at Kingsley, he said to himself. Just like hundreds of other intercepts he had practiced. All he had to do was rely on his training.

"Oakgrove," Rick called on the radio. "Tundra One is lead-nose, Two has the lead, bogey dope."

"Oakgrove copy lead change, understand Tundra One is returning to base."

"Negative, Tundra One is falling into five-mile trail."

"Oakgrove copy trail, bogey now bears tactical one-six-five for forty. Still low. Mission is ID by type and tail number, turn right one-eight-zero, descend and maintain one-zero-thousand."

"Out of three-five-oh for ten-thousand right to one-eight-zero, Tundra Two."

Rick relaxed a little. This shouldn't be too bad. He was going to get close control to the stern. All he had to do was follow the directions of the controller until he was in the stern of the target. Then he could use his radar to move in for the ID.

"Tundra One established five-mile trail," called Dave over the radio.

Good, Rick thought, that was far enough away so he wouldn't have to worry about Dave. Without a radar there really wasn't anything Dave could do, anyway, except offer advice and maybe act as a radio relay.

As if reading his mind, Dave's voice came over the victor radio. "Tundra Two, Tundra One will be maintaining flight level two-five-zero for radio relay."

"Two."

Rick could have kicked himself for not having thought of that in time himself. It was standard procedure. That far out over the Gulf it was hard for the ground controllers to hear radio transmissions from low-flying aircraft. But by keeping one aircraft up high, the two jets in the flight could maintain radio contact with Oakgrove.

As Rick descended, he ran through modes one, two, and four on his interrogator. Each time Rick switched modes and depressed the interrogator button, he looked into the upper left part of his forty-mile radar scope hoping to see the hollow box of a transponder paint. Each time the screen was blank. Whatever was out there, it wasn't a military jet. At least not an American military jet.

As Rick passed through eleven thousand feet, he saw a bright green square about two-thirds of the way down the screen, forty degrees left of his nose.

Rick keyed the radio and spoke, sounding, despite his intentions, rather excited. "Tundra Two, contact forty left, thirty miles, Angels low."

"Contact is target," came the reply from Oakgrove.

Although he planned on running "no-lock" until the final portion of the intercept so he wouldn't set off any radar warning gear the target might have on board, Rick decided to sample lock the target to get a quick hack on its altitude and airspeed. He slewed the acquisition symbols over the target and designated once. By habit, Rick looked up at his HUD to check the weapons parameters for the AIM-7s he always loaded in the simulate mode, even though they weren't on the jet. The HUD showed a good high-aspect shot, but the target was still well out of range.

Glancing down again at his radar scope, Rick updated his call: "Tundra Two locked now, target heading three-six-zero, three hundred and fifty knots, two thousand feet."

Even as Rick said the words he couldn't believe what he was seeing. The target was going 350—no, wait—400 knots. Rick broke the sample lock to avoid giving away his position. "Oakgrove," Rick continued, "I'm showing target accelerating through four hundred knots. Do you concur?"

Oakgrove's reply came weakly through the static, reminding Rick that they were now well offshore. "Oakgrove concur, estimate target five hundred knots."

Five hundred knots. This was no drug runner!

"Tundra, descend and maintain four thousand."

"Tundra."

His pulse quickening, Rick dropped the F-16's nose. Normally he would have pulled the power to keep from gaining too much speed. But against a 500-knot target, he couldn't have too much speed.

His victor radio sparked to life. It was Dave. "Tundra Two," he coached, "you're doing fine. Just remember to keep your speed up."

With his left hand, Rick pushed the throttle up and over the afterburner detent. A slight jump in his altimeter and the *1.1* on his mach meter gave the only indication that he had just gone supersonic.

Dave's voice continued. "Make sure you've fenced in," he directed.

Fence in! Rick had forgotten to fence in—to prepare his weapons systems for possible combat. Correcting his mistake, Rick reached to cool his Sidewinder missiles, arm his flares, and turn on his video recorder. The master arm switch Rick left in the *simulate* position.

"Tundra Two is fenced in," Rick called as he completed the check. He was determined not to dwell on his stupid oversight.

Level at 4,000 feet, Rick saw that the target on his scope was just over twenty miles out. Rick expected a call soon from Oakgrove giving him a final turn to complete the intercept. Turning too late against a fast-moving target might mean an extended tail-chase before Rick could get a visual ID, if, indeed, he could get an ID in the thick clouds.

Just then Dave's voice came again. "Rick," he called, "are you hearing Oakgrove? They just gave you a left turn to zero-nine-zero; they show target maneuvering."

"Negative," Rick replied, "I'm starting left turn now, but I'm not hearing them at all."

Just then Rick did hear something. Something bad. It was a chirp—like a cricket, but a cricket which Rick had never heard when training against F-16s, F-15s, and F-18s. Rick looked up to his radar warning receiver. There, plain as day, at the twelve o'clock position was a *wingform bravo.* He was locked by a Slotback, the air-to-air radar used in the latest Russian-built fighters.

This wasn't supposed to be happening.

"Two's spiked left ten o'clock," Rick practically screamed into his mask. It was a terrifying thought. Whatever it was knew Rick was there and had targeted him.

No longer needing to remain covert, Rick locked the target and pulled his nose around to point at his adversary. The bogey was twenty miles out, slightly below him. The radar target designator box was visible over the aircraft, but the darkness and the clouds made that of little value.

Rick's mind raced. What should he do? He could keep the nose on and force a high aspect pass for the ID. Or, he could go defensive and take the target to the beam—chaffing as he went—to defend against a possible radar missile. But the mission wasn't to be defensive. The mission was to ID.

Dave's voice came in calm over the radio. "Two, say again. Understand spiked?"

"Affirm," Rick called. "I've got him on the nose for fifteen miles. Tell Oakgrove!"

"Oakgrove," relayed Dave, "Target is locked to Tundra Two! Say mission!"

"Oakgrove says mission ID," called Dave.

The range had closed to fifteen miles. If the bogey were going to fire a missile, it would have to do so in the next few seconds. Otherwise Rick would be inside its minimum range.

Rick held his breath, eyeing his radar warning receiver for an indication of a missile launch. If it came, he'd have to defeat the missile, that was all, and then work his way back to the stern. But then what? The target was going supersonic now. If Rick passed 180 degrees out, even if he did get an ID—which he probably wouldn't because of the weather—he'd have to turn all the way around back to the north. He'd never catch the bogey then, and he'd certainly be out of AIM-9 range, even if he got permission to shoot—which he wouldn't, not in peacetime without an ID and without a hostile act out of the bogey.

But wasn't flying toward the American territorial limit, into sovereign American airspace at 500 knots and locking up American interceptors an act of aggression? Rick certainly thought so. But would the sector director and the director's boss, the commander of NORAD, agree? Of course not, and even if they did, what was the chance of getting the word from them in the next two seconds using a radio relay?

Rick had to think. He didn't know what that aircraft was or why it was headed to Florida, or Atlanta, or Washington, or wherever it was going, but Rick knew it was his mission to stop it—to get it to turn around—or at least to identify it before it penetrated American airspace.

The question was, how? He couldn't shoot it down, legally or physically. In the thick clouds, the seeker head of the AIM-9 was useless. If he had been carrying the AIM-7 radar missiles his HUD was simulating, he could have shot already.

It would have been a perfect shot, right in the heart of the envelope. A no-escape shot. The only problem was that he wasn't carrying AIM-7s.

Then it occurred to him. He might not be carrying AIM-7s, but his adversary didn't know that.

Following the instinct demanded by a thousand knots of closure, Rick mashed down on the red pickle button on the sidestick controller with his right thumb. As he had seen and heard hundreds of times in training, the flight path marker in the HUD flashed and his own radar warning receiver chirped loudly, indicating that his radar was directing constant wave energy to guide an AIM-7.

Just as when he had killed Maggot at Kingsley, the AIM-7 Rick launched with his thumb lived only in the computer brain of his jet. There was no missile in the air, just a feint, the kind that put him smack dab in the middle of the game Colonel Johnson had told him about two long years before.

Nothing in NORAD regulations said he couldn't fire CW energy, just that he couldn't shoot a missile. Besides, hadn't he been trained to make the decisions and take the consequences of his actions? But what would those consequences be?

Time seemed to stop. Rick couldn't answer Dave's calls asking what was going on. He couldn't even breathe. All he could do was stare at the darkness that hid the Unknown Rider.

It was the silence that told Rick he had won. He looked up to his radar warning receiver to confirm the sound. It was blank. The bogey had dropped its lock, turned tail, and was on its way back to wherever it was from.

But Rick's imaginary missile still counted down. Five, four, three, two, one. Impact.

* * *

"Knock-it-off, knock-it-off. Oakgrove directs and authenti-cates knock-it-off," called Dave. "Target is turning southbound and squawking the emergency code."

"Copy Knock-it-off. Do they want us to follow it?"

"Negative. Mission is to return to base."

Rick pulled back the power, flipped on the autopilot and sank down in his seat, aware for the first time that he was soaked with sweat. He was also shaking. It seemed that every nerve in his body was crying out for answers, trying to understand what had just happened.

Had he done the right thing? Yes. Of that he was certain. Because whatever that aircraft was, it had been a threat. And though the decision to push that button hadn't been black and white, his mission was: to defend America from aerial intrud-ers, whatever form they might take.

That was what he had done.

Satisfied, Rick unlatched his mask, wiped the sweat from his face, turned the jet north, and headed for home.

Glossary of Abbreviations

AA .... Aspect Angle
AB.. Afterburner
ACC .... Air Combat Command
ACM .... Air Combat Mode
ADF .... Air Defense Fighter
ADI .... Attitude Director Indicator
AFB.. Air Force Base
AFOQT .... Air Force Officer Qualifying Test
AGL .... Above Ground Level
AIM.. Air Intercept Missile
AMRAAM ... Advanced Medium Range Air-to-Air Missile
AMS ....Academy of Military Science
ANG .... Air National Guard
AOA ....Angle of Attack
ATC .... Air Traffic Control/Air Training Command
ATIS .... Automatic Terminal Information Service
BFM .... Basic Fighter Maneuvers
BVR ....Beyond Visual Range
CAP .... Combat Air Patrol
C-BITS ....Computer Based Instruction and Testing
CDI ....Course Deviation Indicator
CG .... Center of Gravity
CI... Course Indicator
DACT .... Dissimilar Air Combat Training
DITY..Do It Yourself
DNIF .... Duty Not Involving Flying
EID .... Electronic Identification
EOR .... End of Runway
EPU... Emergency Power Unit
FAIP .... First Assignment Instructor Pilot
FCC .... Fire Control Computer
FCNP .... Fire Control Navigation Computer

Glossary, continued

FEB .... Flight Evaluation Board
FISHPOT .... Flight Screening Program Officer Training
FLCS .... Flight Control System
FTIT .... Fan Turbine Inlet Temperature
GCI .... Ground Controlled Intercept
GLOC .... G-induced Loss Of Consciousness
HSI .... Horizontal Situation Indicator
HUD .... Heads Up Display
INS .... Inertial Navigation System
IP .... Instructor Pilot
JFS .... Jet Fuel Starter
MDC .... Modern Day Cowboy
MiG ... Mikoyan Gureyvich (Soviet Aircraft Designator)
MIL .... Military Power
                                    (maximum non-afterburner power)
MOA .... Military Operations Area
NAS .... Naval Air Station
NASA .... National Aeronautics and
                                                    Space Administration
NORAD .... North American Aerospace Defense
NORDO .... No Operative Radio
NWS .... Nose Wheel Steering
OTS .... Officer Training School
REO .... Radar Electrical Optical
RMI .... Radio Magnetic Indicator
ROE .... Rules of Engagement
RWR .... Radar Warning Receiver
SA .... Situational Awareness
SFO .... Simulated Flameout Approach
SHP .... Student Harassment Program
SIM .... Simulator
TAC .... Tactical Air Command
TACAN .... Tactical Air Navigation
TLA .... Three Letter Acronym
UPT .... Undergraduate Pilot Training
VID .... Visual Identification
VMC .... Visual Meteorological Conditions
VTR .... Video Tape Recorder
VVI .... Vertical Velocity Indicator
WEZ .... Weapons Employment Zone
WSO .... Weapons Systems Operator

Scott Anderson is an F-16 Air Defense Pilot with the Minnesota Air National Guard. He holds degrees in Mechanical Engineering and History from Stanford University and is the author of Distant Fires, *1991 American Library Association Best Book for Young Adults.* Unknown Rider *is his first novel.*